CS-nt

23/5

Birthing Work

"In this fantastic contribution, Katharine McKinnon provides mothers, birthing professionals and academics stuck in the 'birth wars' with tools to unpack the birthing experience. Readers will be enthralled with the wide array of options to negotiate the birthing space and process. *Birthing Work* is filled with gripping stories, of McKinnon's own birthing experiences and that of a range of women and birthing professionals. This is a must read for all those involved in the work of child birth."

—Gerda Roelvink, *author of* Building Dignified Worlds:
Geographies of Collective Action

"This book doesn't just nudge old debates about birth in different directions; it spurs them into entirely new territory prompting readers to consider how humans and more-than-humans assemble around birth. Weaving together stories and conversations with mothers, midwives and doctors, Katherine McKinnon highlights the diversity of experiences of childbirth, resisting any singular universal truth. Babies, bodies, beds, institutions, machines and clocks act collectively to shape pregnancy and birth, enabling a range of different processes to unfold. *Birthing Work* is an important volume for human geographers but also for anyone interested in radically rethinking childbirth, labour and love."

—Robyn Longhurst, *Deputy Vice-Chancellor Academic and Professor
of Geography, University of Waikato, New Zealand*

"This small book about birth is a gold mine of observations, reflections and conjectures about the terrain of human birth. The terrain of childbirth is a disputed territory in our society. Dr. McKinnon describes all the players, both animate and inanimate, in that disputed terrain. The book goes beyond the disputes and offers rich insights into the many corners of childbirth. The book draws on the experience of individuals; it draws on several disciplines, including midwifery, obstetrics, philosophy, biology, sociology, human geography and quantitative epidemiology and thereby suggests ways of thinking and acting beyond our current constraints."

—Andrew Bisits, *Obstetrician, Maternity Medical Co-Director at Royal Hospital
for Women, and Conjoint Associate Professor at UNSW School of Women
and Children's Health*

Katharine McKinnon

Birthing Work

The Collective Labour of Childbirth

Katharine McKinnon
Department of Social Inquiry
La Trobe University
Bendigo, VIC, Australia

ISBN 978-981-15-0009-1   ISBN 978-981-15-0010-7   (eBook)
https://doi.org/10.1007/978-981-15-0010-7

Cover illustration: © John Rawsterne/patternhead.com

This Palgrave Pivot imprint is published by the registered company Springer Nature
Singapore Pte Ltd.
The registered company address is: 152 Beach Road, #21-01/04 Gateway East, Singapore
189721, Singapore

PREFACE

As a mother of three, I have muddled my way through pregnancy and birth in three different places, with three different sets of doctors and midwives. Each time I had to make, and remake, decisions about tests and scans, about how to manage work commitments, care for my changing body, my children, my home, whether and what kind of medications to take or not take, what kind of food to eat, what kind of breastfeeding/ swaddling/baby transport/toileting paraphernalia to commit to. Each of these involved some degree of choice and some expression of the values my partner and I hold around pregnancy, birth and childrearing. This project began in the year following the birth of my second daughter at a time when I felt acutely dissatisfied with the intellectual resources available to me as I navigated the sticky spaces of parental decision-making. I wanted something other than moralising discourses about 'right' or 'wrong' choices, the pervasive sense of mother-blame, or the false neutrality of the clinical-sounding language that seemed to infuse so much of the information available to me. It is with this dissatisfaction that this project was born, and, equally, with a desire to find language for the experience of childbearing, an experience that is both deeply profound and profoundly hard work. In this book, I hope to both honour that profound experience and provide some new ways of thinking about what the work of childbirth is and what it means to do that work.

It is always the case that a researcher, an author, is implicated in the design and the findings of the research. Objectivity is always an impossibility. But in the case of this project, I have been more deeply and more personally implicated in the subject matter than ever before. In this book, I have worked to put my own commitments to one side and write from the stories that women shared with us in interviews. I have endeavoured to be true to their views and experiences. But I also acknowledge that there is no way to take a completely neutral position either. This is one reason why each chapter begins with a story taken from my own experiences of childbirth. These were written as I reflected on my births and sought moments that spoke to the themes of that chapter. This is part an acknowledgement that my interest in the issue of childbirth is as much personal as professional, part a desire to connect with readers at an emotional as well as intellectual level, and in part an effort to enact something I've elsewhere called 'naked scholarship' (McKinnon, 2017): an attempt to work as an academic with an open heart, to make clear my own cares and concerns, while creating a space where the related cares and concerns of others can also stand strong.

When we write things down we are always telling a story, and stories do an unavoidable violence to the messy complicated smudginess of embodied everyday life. Narratives tidy everything up, creating order and meaning. And this always requires an exclusion of something, a decision to make some part of that reality invisible or unimportant. Academic texts are particularly skilful in this regard, as they are often written from the voice of authority, the knowingness of the expert. In these texts there is little room for the flawed, fuller, humanity of the speaker to be heard. I have sought to write this book in a different kind of voice—one that, I hope, begins to practise open-heartedness and emotional connection as a value even within academic texts. I also have sought to make this text accessible to readers outside my field of human geography, thus keeping discussions of theory to a minimum, and attempting to purge the text of unnecessary jargon.

There are many people to thank along the way, not least of all the daughter with whom I began this journey and whose fierce love and gentle heart are a daily revelation. It was the kind and wise guidance of our Sydney midwife, Jane Palmer, who helped to initiate my curiosity about why the options for maternity care were so different between Australia and New Zealand. With support from a Macquarie University Return from Parental Leave grant in 2011, I was able to speak with mothers, midwives, and obstetricians in both countries to explore it further. This book has slowly taken shape in fits and starts through the years since, much of it written in the beautiful surrounds of the Convento S. Maria del Giglio in Bolsena, Italy during writing retreats supported by the Julie Graham Community Economies Research Fund and the nurturing contributions of folk in the Community Economies Collective who gave generous readings of early drafts, offered provocative feedback, contributed to shared thinking and encouragement. I am indebted in particular to two members of that Collective: Kelly Dombroski and Stephen Healy, with whom I have shared this intellectual journey over the past few years and whose phenomenally deep and creative intellects I admire enormously. All of what I have to say is indebted to the conversation shared with them over the years, and both are shadow authors of this text.

There are many others to whom I owe a debt of gratitude for their contributions and support over the years. The wonderful women and men who were willing to share their stories, the many friends and acquaintances who have offered their ideas and asked challenging questions as the work has taken shape. Audiences at the talks I have given whose interest and engagement has been a vital encouragement and source of critical reflection. In particular I want to acknowledge the contributions of the team of reviewers who have helped me: the anonymous reviewers who gave such encouraging response and guidance; the hardworking Ph.D. students—Caitlin Finlayson and Melissa Kennedy—who kindly made time to read it; my 'community readers'—Affrika McCarthy, Cath Ryan, Ronnie Moule and Linda Malam—for their insightful and often heartwarming comments on earlier drafts of this manuscript; Raffaella and Lucia who struggled through the adult language to give their thumbs up to the stories of their births; and my intellectual mentors in the Community Economies Collective, particularly Katherine Gibson and Stephen Healy, whose critical insights on early drafts were pivotal in helping the whole thing to take shape.

Finally, none of this writing would have been possible without the patient and loving support of my family—especially Marco, Lucia, Raffaella and Frederica—and our incredible network of friends who have taken care of children, shared meals, provided transport, offered kind words and solidarity, asked questions, and given much-needed hugs. I am deeply thankful for my great fortune in being part of such a marvellous community of family, friends, and colleagues.

Bendigo, Australia   Katharine McKinnon

Reference

McKinnon, K. (2017). Naked scholarship: Prefiguring a new world through uncertain development geographies. *Geographical Research, 55*(3), 344–349. https://doi.org/10.1111/1745-5871.12196.

CONTENTS

CHAPTER 1

Introduction: Assembling Birth

Abstract This chapter introduces the idea of the childbirth assemblage at the core of the book, introducing how closer attention to the multiplicity of actors involved in childbirth could provide a pathway to exit the birth wars, and a way to rethink care-work more generally. The so-called 'birth wars' have created a maternity care context immersed in highly charged, moralistic and competitive debates about what is the 'right' way to have a baby. In this context, many women and their families become haunted by rightness or wrongness of the choices they have made or circumstances they have been forced into, and carers and families alike are caught in apparently irreconcilable adversarial clash between two sides. This chapter introduces the idea that just as important as choice is the recognition that from the beginning of pregnancy, childbearing brings us into new conversations with human and more-than-human others who play an active role in pregnancy and childbirth, and who together, form a childbirth assemblage that undertakes maternal work.

Keywords Assemblage · Choice · Birth wars · Care · Maternal work

I have given birth three times and was born once myself. The first birth I do not remember, but legend has it I was in a hurry and shot out of my mother's body to be caught just in time by the obstetrician in her mustard yellow sari, still pulling on her rubber apron and gloves. That was on a stainless steel hospital

© The Author(s) 2020
K. McKinnon, *Birthing Work*,
https://doi.org/10.1007/978-981-15-0010-7_1

bed in Suva, Fiji. When I first gave birth myself I had chosen a homebirth. This was in New Zealand, where midwives are usually the 'lead maternity carer' through pregnancy, often working across hospital and home settings. That was a long, slow birth, and I found myself at the end, wheeled into hospital and led onto a hospital bed where my feet were strapped into stirrups. The just-in-time crowning of my daughter was all that stopped me from an unwanted (and unnecessary) episiotomy from the doctor who leaned in with a scalpel and asked permission by saying "I'll just give you a little cut". Thank goodness for Lucia's awesome sense of dramatic timing. The second time I gave birth was in Australia, where, in trying to find a midwife who would be my lead carer, I had few options. Lucky to have a secure academic income, I was able to pay for an independent midwife and gave birth at home in a lovely warm pool. For a moment I thought 'I can't do this,' but my midwife whispered 'You can, you are,' and the next moment I was lifting my second daughter out through the water where Raffaella nestled back down to sleep, without uttering a sound. But it was during my last birth that I finally understood we were a team, baby and I, as I felt her turn into the birth canal and push herself out with her feet. That was Frederica, and she arrived in three pushes as the 11.45 am Maldon steam engine blew its whistle at the station.

My experiences are by no means unusual, but what is distinctive is that giving birth under two different maternity care systems gave me insight into the sometimes stark contrasts between the two. When I sought care during my second pregnancy in Australia, I encountered for the first time the so-called 'birth wars' (MacColl, 2009) in which advocates of natural birth are pitted against those aligned with a technocratic (Davis-Floyd, 2001) or medicalised approach. The one side believe firmly that a woman's body is designed to give birth and should be interfered with as little as possible, enabling what is termed 'normal' physiological birth. The other side focus less on the conditions that would allow normal birth to occur, and more on the potential risks involved. Thus, the medicalised approach involves much more routine use of medical technologies and is quicker to intervene. In New Zealand, while these debates are present, there is not such a stark division between the two sides, and it is possible to remain within the state-funded maternity care system while planning for a midwife-attended homebirth. In Australia the public health care system is very different. In Australia I was forced to make a much more radical decision. If I wanted the care of a midwife, and I wanted the midwife I saw during pregnancy to be the one attending my birth, then I had little choice but to pay for the services of an independent midwife, and run the gauntlet of disapproving

GPs and hospital staff when I went for the standard series of tests and scans. I lived in Sydney at the time, and for a city of 4.5 million, there were only 8 independent midwives. My experiences of these contrasts sparked a curiosity about why things were so different and, more importantly, how women were being affected as the birth wars shaped their experiences of childbirth. As a social scientist, and a human geographer, my scholarship is committed to the Marxist tradition in which the point of research is to understand the way things are so that they might change. And so, I began an ethnographic study intended to cut across the polarised debates.

In an effort to sidestep the birth wars, I thought to ask women to share their birth stories, while creating an inventory of the many different people and things that inhabited the birth space and had a role to play in shaping that space and women's experiences of birth. The idea was to flesh out the complexities and multiplicities of birth experiences, against a context in which women and carers are expected to take sides. My bedside reading during that second pregnancy, in which I first encountered the Australian maternity care system, was Jane Bennett's *Vibrant Matter* (2010). Bennett opened up the idea that a thing—a spool of thread, a plastic cup—has power and agency. The sense that *things* have power spoke to my experience at the time: inhabiting a pregnant body that felt no longer quite my own; interacting regularly with scales and measuring tapes and urine testing sticks that seemed to mediate the relationship between me and the growing baby; having to (re)learn very different ways of inhabiting the world, whether it was the narrow hallways at work, my ability to ride a bicycle, or the piles of cushions I needed to enable me to sleep at night. The idea that material objects, inanimate things, and my own sensing-feeling body had an active role to play in the world resonated. My exploration of *Birthing Work* was sparked in conversation with these ideas, and is an attempt to take Bennett's challenge into the experience of childbirth, to explore 'what things do' in the spaces in which women give birth.

Bennett's work sits alongside a larger literature that questions the human-centric focus of much social science and seeks instead to engage with how human societies sit alongside, within, and in intimate relations with, a range of non-human others. The work of Bruno Latour, Annemarie Mol and John Law, for example, emphasises the ways in which human actors do things in tandem with non-human actors.[1] This approach, often

---

[1] Mol and Law, for example, have investigated how diabetes comes into existence through human experiences and self-awareness of daily symptoms, through the scientific knowledge

presented under the banner 'Actor Network Theory' (ANT), prioritises a form of sociological analysis that begins by being attentive to the relationships formed between people and things in ways that make certain kinds of actions possible.[2] In the context of pregnancy and childbirth, there is a lot of pressure to make the 'right' decision about care (or testing, or where you give birth, or what you eat, or how you exercise, or whether you find out the sex of the baby—the anxiety-provoking list goes on). Paying attention to the role that things play offered a way to explore the experience of childbirth in a different way, and I was curious to discover what such an approach would uncover.

In this book I start to figure out what happens if we take seriously what these 'things' do and the ways that they are put to work in making a birth. I explore how the experience of childbirth is made up of the shared work that things and people do, the way childbirth is 'assembled' from the conjoint, and often collaborative, efforts of all of these actors. Focusing on the diversity of actors engaged in the birth space is one way to get past the often paralysing debates around birth (and health care more broadly) that hinge on questions of making the 'right' choices over maternity care—but it does not preclude the need to think about how we, collectively, could do more to enable childbirth amidst loving kindness.

Getting Past the Birth Wars

The need to think about kindness and love in childbirth is something that deserves to be taken seriously. More than 90% of women worldwide will give birth at some point in their lifetime. While it only takes a short interval of time in a woman's life, it is a deeply affecting and profound experience. A woman's experience of birth can shape her mental, emotional and physical wellbeing, her capacity to care for her child. Not only this, but *how* a child is born has implications for their future health and development. New clinical research indicates that the care women receive before, during, and after birth has a profound and lasting impact on the health and

---

that unravel the characteristics of diabetes as a *condition*, and through the technologies and instruments that enable detection, monitoring, and regulation of that condition (Mol, 2008; Mol & Law, 2004).

[2] See ANT, discussed at length in Latour (2005) and Law (2004).

wellbeing of both parents and babies.[3] It also shapes the experiences of subsequent pregnancies and labour, with some women rejecting the health system altogether after experiences of bullying or trauma during care.[4]

In Australia and the United States (as well as many other places), the majority of birthing mothers will encounter a maternity care system immersed in highly charged, moralistic, and competitive debates about what is the 'right' way to have a baby. In this context, many women and their families become haunted by rightness or wrongness of the choices they have made, or circumstances they have been forced into, and carers and families alike are caught in apparently irreconcilable clash between two sides. In her account of the failings of the maternity care system in Australia, MacColl (2009) identifies many of the problems as the result of an unresolved 'birth war', where midwives and obstetricians, advocates of natural birth, and advocates of medical approaches, seem unable to get beyond their conflict in order to focus on providing the care that mothers need.

On one side are those who argue that the optimal way to give birth harnesses the natural processes of a woman's body to birth without medical intervention (the obstetric term for this is 'normal birth'). GP and author Sarah Buckley terms this 'undisturbed birth':

Undisturbed birth represents the smoothest hormonal orchestration of the birth process, and therefore the easiest transition possible; physiologically, hormonally, psychologically, and emotionally, from pregnancy and birth to new motherhood and lactation, for each woman. When a mother's hormonal

---

[3] Researchers are concerned that babies born to mothers who are prevented from experiencing normal labour carry the negative microbiological and epigenetic impacts of this through their lives (Dahlen, Downe, Kennedy, & Foureur, 2014; Dahlen et al., 2013).

[4] One third of women experience trauma during childbirth, due to treatment that is coercive, bullying, disrespectful, or even violent, and there are rising rates of Post-Traumatic Stress Disorder (PTSD) in women following birth (Simpson, Schmied, Dickson, & Dahlen, 2018). Post-traumatic stress contributes to rising rates of postnatal depression and maternal morbidity due to suicide (Thornton, Schmied, Dennis, Barnett, & Dahlen, 2013). Such trauma is also associated with low self-esteem and disrupted family relationships, and difficulties with mother–child bonding that can impact a child's social, emotional and mental development (Reed, Sharman, & Inglis, 2017). Maternity care systems suffer from the prevalence of a culture of bullying in obstetrics (Paice & Smith, 2009) and an unacceptable use of force against women, something now termed obstetric violence (Kitzinger, 2006; Pérez D'Gregorio, 2010; Sadler et al., 2016). Against this backdrop, increasing numbers of women, at least in Australia, are choosing to opt out of the system and 'freebirth' or homebirth against medical advice (Dahlen, Jackson, & Stevens, 2011; Feeley & Thomson, 2016; Jackson, Dahlen, & Schmied, 2012).

> orchestration is undisturbed, her baby's safety is also enhanced, not only during labour and birth, but also in the critical postnatal transition from womb to world. (Buckley, 2011)

Undisturbed birth, as described by Buckley, is difficult to obtain in most hospital settings due to the routine use of foetal heart rate monitors, internal examination of labouring women, bright lights, steady traffic of clinical staff, and administration of synthetic hormones to women whose labours are progressing slowly. Yet for advocates of what is sometimes termed 'medicalised' birth, the monitors, regulation of progress, and examinations, are a necessary part of keeping women and babies safe, and enabling doctors to intervene early if things are going wrong. The medical model is focused on the prevention of adverse outcomes, and on predicting and managing risk, and treating complications during pregnancy and childbirth. The focus on risk prevention also tends to 'emphasize the use of testing, coupled with the use of medical or surgical interventions to avert a poor outcome' (OBOS Pregnancy and Birth Contributors, 2014). Such interventions are understood to be a vital part of modern maternity care and are often necessary. The concern however, is that the medical model puts so much emphasis on clinical risk management that those trained in this model lack the skills to support a natural birth.

In contrast, those interested in undisturbed birth place much more emphasis on respect and rights, and a concern for a joyous, affirming and empowering birth for mother and baby. Midwife and long-time advocate for natural birth, Ina May Gaskin, typifies this perspective:

> Women's perceptions about their bodies and their babies' capabilities will be deeply influenced by the care they receive around the time of their birth… Giving birth can be the most empowering experience of a lifetime - an initiation into a new dimension of mind-body awareness - or it can be disempowering, by removing from new mothers any sense of inner strength or capacity …. Birth may be followed by an empowering joy, a euphoria that they will never forget, or by a depression than can make the mother a stranger to herself and everyone who knows her. (Gaskin, 2011, pp. 1–2)

A mother's feelings of safety are understood by Gaskin and by Buckley to be an important factor in both helping a birth unfold safely and naturally, and in setting a mother up for competent caregiving.

The World Health Organization agrees with Gaskin that it is critical that giving birth is not only a safe but also a positive experience for mothers and families, something that is achieved under a woman-centred model of care (World Health Organization, 2018). A woman-centred model highlights the importance of empowered birth, supporting normal birth, and a continuity of care model in which a woman has the opportunity to build trusting relationships with the carers who will support her during childbirth. Much midwifery research lends support to this approach and warns against the potential harm that women are experiencing as a result of contemporary practices in hospital-based maternity care. As the World Health Organization recognises, while in some parts of the world 'too few interventions are being provided too late to women, in other settings women are receiving too many interventions that they do not need too soon' (World Health Organization, 2018). The worry of those who advocate for women-centred care is that too many women in the developed world are experiencing the latter.

What is widely presented as a solution to this problem at present, is that women would be able to make choices about their care: they should be able to choose where to go, who to see, what position to take during labour and birth, whether to accept an episiotomy or allow themselves to tear, and to have access to the information that would allow them to make informed decisions about all this and more. I worry, however, that 'choice' may not be enough.

THE CHILDBIRTH ASSEMBLAGE

This research sought to cut across the polarising debates about birth (home/hospital; natural/medical; midwifery/obstetrics; risky/safe; empowering/clinical) by turning our attention to the diversity of birth experience and the diversity of actors within the birth space. Focusing on diversity focuses attention beyond the entrenched debates of the birth wars. It also helped my co-researchers and me to move beyond the personal values that informed our own decisions about childbirth and the decisions we made in relation to the births of our own children.

The focus on diversity has been informed by scholarship of a 'pluriversal' world (Escobar, 2018; Gibson-Graham et al., 2017): in the context of childbirth this means a world in which there is no simple right or wrong, but a range of legitimate practices and experience, and multiple pathways towards bringing new life into the world. What is being practised here is an effort to 'look for difference' in the face of hegemony,[5] a methodological strategy of looking for the ways things do not always 'line up' with dominant accounts. In this case, looking for difference involves a refusal to be co-opted by either side of the birth wars binary. This is not to say that 'anything goes' or that there are not ethical dilemmas in birth, or that some things ought not to be more valued than others. Rather, what a pluriversal view of the experience of childbirth highlights is that some practices make the work of childbirth easier, some allow it to happen amidst loving kindness, while others make it happen in the thick of fear and powerlessness—in many cases, the experience is a blend.

To understand something of the range of experiences, Kelly Dombroski, myself, and research assistant Robyn Short, spoke with 29 mothers, 11 mid-wives and 4 obstetricians in Australia and New Zealand.[6] We approached interviews as a guided conversation (Gudeman & Rivera, 1995), during which we asked our participants to share their experiences of childbirth and describe the rooms within which the work of childbirth took place. Participants self-selected to take part in the interviews, responding either to leaflets circulated through online networks or by 'snowballing,' where one respondent would recommend another. This means we only spoke to mothers who wanted to share their stories, and to midwives and obstetricians who were willing to be asked about their practice. The cultural diversity of our respondents was limited: the majority were white Australians or Pakeha, but we also spoke with women of Lebanese, Chinese, and Maori backgrounds.

Among our participants were women who told stories of being trauma-tised during their labours and bullied by the obstetricians and midwives who were supposed to be caring for them. Some of these women made the decision subsequently to birth at home, either under the care of a quali-fied midwife (homebirth) or alone (freebirth). Also among our participants

---

[5] Looking for difference is one of the methodologies used by J. K. Gibson-Graham and others who form part of the 'Community Economic Collective' (Gibson-Graham, 2006; Gibson-Graham et al., 2017; Gibson-Graham, Cameron, & Healy, 2013). It is based on the work of Eve Sedgewick and her critique of the 'Christmas effect'.

[6] Partners have a very important role in the birth space, and it has been suggested that when fathers began to be permitted to stay with their wives during childbirth, many of the brutal-ities associated with hospital practices in the mid-twentieth century began to be challenged (although Odent (2009) argues that the presence of stressed-out fathers has had a largely negative effect on childbirth). In this study, however, we did not seek to recruit partners and only one partner joined our interviews to give his perspective.

were women who strongly rejected the idea of 'natural birth,' and sought a more controlled and predictable delivery by planned caesarean. For many women their birth experiences and philosophies of birth lay in the broad spectrum between these extremes. In this book I hope to honour these diverse stories and perspectives. This would not be possible if the only way to understand these women's experiences was in relation to the ongoing skirmishes and battles of the birth wars, or questions of what is necessarily 'good' or 'right' in birth.

In the interviews, we asked participants to identify what had been in that space with them, including the birth attendants and support people, the furniture and equipment, and the intangible expectations and policies: in short, the rich collection of people and things that all had a role to play. In creating such an inventory, and asking respondents to name that which had been most important and why, we constructed a picture of the diversity of things (people, objects, beliefs, practices, institutions, feelings) that contribute to the experience of childbirth. This catalogue provided the foundations for an understanding of birth based on knowing its diversity and multiplicity.

A brief inventory of workers in the birth spaces provides immediate insight into the diversity and multiplicity of childbirth, and the interdependencies that are crucial to that space. Imagine the mother at the centre of what will become a complex web of connections and interconnections between her and those that gather around as she labours. Now add the *baby* who is within her, but who has his own role to play. What position the baby moves himself into, whether she is ready to be born, how his emotions fare during labour and birth all have a role to play. Now consider the relationships that come into being a mother-to-be and her carers, including perhaps an *obstetrician*, who she may have chosen and paid, to help her to safely bring her baby into the world. The obstetrician carries an arsenal of prior experience and training. The obstetrician's work is regulated by *hospital policy* and, in some settings, by the conditions of the indemnity *insurance* they are required to carry. Insurance policies are in turn determined by *actuaries* who assign probability and dollar values to risk. The obstetrician relies upon the work of *midwives* who will support a woman through her labour, and unless something begins to go wrong, the obstetrician may not even enter the room—it is the midwife's training to care for normal birth, and the obstetrician's training to provide care when something goes wrong. So far, the work these actors do is fairly legible, they are professionals doing what they are paid to do.

The assessments of risk that determine policy, determine in turn an obstetrician's clinical decision-making. And here is where it begins to get more complicated. Emotions have a role to play in any decision, and (as I will elaborate in Chapter 5) if a risk-averse obstetrician is feeling stressed or afraid, that will shape decisions in a particular way. Here we are no longer dealing with the familiar work of the health professional, but the work being done within the human body. Fear might be working within the doctor's *limbic system* to shape particular decisions. And fear is infectious. A fear that is passed on to the mother will affect her *hormones* (releasing *adrenaline*, inhibiting *oxytocin*—the hormone that is released when we feel love and which body produces during labour). This in turn affects her labour and her baby. A mother's fear and the body's release of adrenaline can slow down labour as *muscles* fail to contract (Buckley, 2005, 2015).

When labour slows down, hospital-based midwives who are caring for the mother through labour become concerned with the 'failure to progress' and introduce synthetic oxytocin (*Pitocin* or *Syntocinon*) to help speed things up. These synthetic hormones usually create intense contractions, inhibit the body's production of natural oxytocin, and thus lead to a significant increase in *pain*. To relieve the pain, an *epidural* is often recommended, which in turn slows down labour. The drugs administered through epidural can also cause distress to the baby, which is detected through the *Cardiotocogram (CTG)* that may be monitoring his heart rate, and carers are left with little option but to suggest a caesarean section. This is known as 'cascade of interventions' and involves introducing an increasing number of actors, including the *anaesthetist* who delivers the pain relief, and the pharmaceutical companies who test and supply the drugs. The end result of the cascade is usually a woman on a *bed*, wheeled into an operating *theatre*, and an obstetrician wielding a *scalpel*. Now the web of connections includes people (mother, baby, obstetrician, anaesthetist, actuary), institutions (hospital, insurance companies, actuarial companies), emotions and sensations (fear, pain), technologies (CTG, epidural, scalpel), biophysical elements (hormones, limbic system). And this is only to name a few of the different actors involved.

The labour involved in birth is physical, emotional, and more. And it is not just humans who do this work, it is the network of sub-human, more-than-human, other-than-human things that assemble around a birth, enabling different kinds of processes and procedures to unfold. Taken together these actors constitute what I am calling a childbirth assemblage— together they contribute to the collective task of birthing babies.

MATERNAL WORK

As the transcribed interviews were read through, and the inventory compiled of who and what took part in shaping birth experiences, what emerged was a picture of the complex diversity of who (and what) does *the work* of childbirth. It is the work not just of the mother, or of her midwife or obstetrician. It is the work of many: not only the woman who labours, but, gathered around her and within her, hormones that help (or hinder) labour, various instruments and machinery, emotions of anticipation, love, and fear, lights that blind and darkness that protects, music that soothes and a bed that holds. There are also; the will and readiness of the baby, the guiding power of hospital policies, the training and ethics of birth attendants, and the pharmaceutical and insurance companies that lay out and constrain options. And the list could go on.

In seeking to honour the diversity of women's experiences and recognise the interconnected actors that shape childbirth, I am taking a deliberate stance against what theorist Julie Stephens calls 'postmaternal thinking'. As Stephens details, postmaternal thinking is one of the hallmarks of contemporary market ideologies which value self-sufficiency to the point of obliterating ideals linked to 'maternal forms of care and the figure of the nurturing mother' (Stephens, 2011, p. xii). Under this regime, everything maternal has been relegated to the private sphere, producing the kinds of anxieties that plague mothers forced to confront the impossible contradictions between a public sphere that only values them for their economic productivity and a private sphere in which they are meant to take on sole responsibility for mothering. The symptoms are well known, as elaborated in journalist Annabelle Crabb's witty account of *The Wife Drought* (2014). The postmaternal is unrepentantly individualistic, envisioning an 'unencumbered, self-sufficient, rational, and freely choosing agent [that is] the antithesis of maternal notions of subjectivity' (Stephens, 2011, p. 7). While our society seems to value independence and economic productivity above all else, it is dependency and care—the values of the maternal—that must be attended to first in life. As anthropologist James Ferguson argues, 'before a man can produce, he must be nursed—...the receipt of unconditional and unearned distribution and care must always precede any productive labour' (Ferguson, 2015, p. 45). It is the interdependency bound up in the work of maternal care that I am interested in here.

It is relatively unusual to think about childbirth as a form of work. While it is commonly said that labour and childbirth is 'hard work', there is little philosophical consideration of what that work is or what it means. A handful of feminist scholars of reproductive labour have, in the past, explored childbirth as a form of labour. These explorations tend to have been subsumed within an investigation of the patriarchal structuring of society and the way childbearing has shaped women's oppression (Russel, 1997). Applying Marxist analysis of the productive labour process, both Mary O'Brien (1981) and Kathryn Russel (1997) proposed that childbearing should be regarded as labour because it fit Marx's definition of human labour as a 'productive activity of a definite kind, carried on with a definite aim' (*Capital*, 1977, 133, cited by Russel). Russel and O'Brien both assert that procreation and childbirth is one such activity, pointing out that women regulate, plan, and consciously engage with the bodily processes and experiences of pregnancy and childbirth, and that, similar to other forms of labour, childbirth is mediated by social relations. Thus, Russel argues, childbirth must also be regarded as 'concrete, useful labour because it is a definite form of activity carried out to achieve a definite aim. It can be undertaken to produce use values, ones needed by others' (p. 334).

These limited explorations place the labour of childbirth and childrearing clearly under the heading of 'reproductive labour'. Reproductive labour is commonly defined as the work associated with tasks of reproducing human life, building and maintaining the workforce that was needed to ensure a continuity of material production. Silvia Federici includes in this category 'all the activities necessary for the reproduction of human life—from housework to subsistence agriculture, to the production of culture and care for the environment' (Federici, 2012, p. 55). In this book I do not use the term 'reproductive work', in part because the 'reproductive' is always understood in relation to its more visible and more valued other, 'productive' work. In this binary relation there is always a tussle between which one is more important, and which comes first. In daily life and the messy stitching together of livelihoods, the lived reality is that all of these activities are important and productive, whether or not they produce a wage (Morrow & Dombroski, 2015). In the context of a childbirth assemblage such distinctions are not particularly helpful. The work required in childbirth is better supported, I would argue, by an understanding of the conscious, effortful, and interdependent labours of all who gather, regardless of whether their contributions might be categorised as productive, reproductive, or other. For lack of a better term, this is something I am calling maternal work, and this book is an attempt to unravel what that work looks like in the spaces of childbirth.

Conclusion

The best we seem to be able to hope for in our maternity care systems at the moment is to be given the freedom to choose—to choose what kind of care we want to receive, where we want to have our baby, whether or not we are induced, and so on. Choice is important, and even more important, the availability of information and balanced medical opinion upon which to choose. But choice also assumes a mother can be an 'unencumbered, self-sufficient, rational, and freely choosing agent', and it lays on her the burden of making the 'right' choice.[7]

The effort to take seriously the work that 'things' do is intended to move past the paralysing debates around birth (and health care more broadly) that hinge on questions of choice and rational decision-making. The recognition that a multiplicity of factors shape childbirth challenges any claim or false expectation that one person can be in charge of what unfolds in the birth space. And it is a way of beginning to find a different language that allows us to value appropriately the diverse kinds of work done to bring new life into the world. The baby, the mother, their limbic systems working in tune, the midwives that encourage, the partner that gives love, the muscles that contract, the bed that supports her, the water that comforts her... all these things together do the work of childbirth.

In contrast to the emphasis on choice, I am interested in exploring how, from the beginning of pregnancy, childbearing brings us into new conversations with one another and necessitates the formation of new relationships. These are new relationships with ourselves, with our partners and families, with those who care for us through pregnancy and childbirth, and with the child to be born. They are also relationships with others who are more-than or other-than human: objects, bodies, technologies. In this book I explore this assemblage of actors, consider what our relationships with them means for childbirth, and how closer attention to them could provide not only a pathway to exit the birth wars, but perhaps a way to rethink care-work more generally.

The book explores these pathways through a series of six chapters, focusing on just a handful of the actors that do work in a childbirth assemblage. When the interviews with mothers, midwives, and obstetricians were taken as a whole, there were key players that emerged as important across the

---

[7]See further discussion of the dilemmas of 'choice' in Dombroski, McKinnon, and Healy (2016).

board. These actors crossed boundaries of the intimate and the worldly, and in this book I follow them inwards, to the unborn baby and down to a woman's biochemical responses, and outwards to the actions and inactions of carers, the beeping of machines, the inert furniture, and the vagaries of the institutions that govern birth, with all their policies and procedures. Through the chapters I draw on the stories and experiences that were shared, including sharing my own stories at the beginning of each chapter. These excerpts from transcribed interviews are highlighted in italics to distinguish them from other quotations. Chapter 2 begins with considering the human actors in the room, focusing particularly on the actors who are everyone's central concern, but whose agency is seldom recognised—the baby. Chapter 3 extends the inwards gaze to the way that a woman's body 'works' during childbirth, the complex and delicate nature of that work, and the ways that carers seek to work *with* the body as they assist a woman through childbirth. In Chapter 4 I turn to the objects in the room, focusing on the bed, whose role involves both supporting a woman and enabling intervention. The bed, like the bureaucracies of institutions I consider in Chapter 5, and the technologies that are the focus of Chapter 6, are ubiquitous presences in hospital spaces, and women and their carers navigate childbirth alongside them, sometimes enrolling their assistance, sometimes actively resisting it. In my final empirical chapter, I turn to the role of time, and particularly the role of clock-time, in shaping how childbirth unfolds. With the help of this assembled cast of actors, I seek to unravel the intricate and messy ways in which each of these things does work in the spaces of childbirth, contributing to the collective birthing work through which a child is brought into the world.

References

Bennett, J. (2010). *Vibrant matter: A political ecology of things.* Durham and London: Duke University Press.

Buckley, S. J. (2005). *Gentle birth, gentle mothering.* Brisbane: One Moon Press.

Buckley, S. J. (2011). Undisturbed birth. *AIMS Journal, 23*(4). Retrieved from https://www.aims.org.uk/journal/item/undisturbed-birth.

Buckley, S. J. (2015). *Hormonal physiology of childbearing: Evidence and implications for women, babies, and maternity care.* Washington, DC: Childbirth Connection Programs, National Partnership for Women & Families.

Crabb, A. (2014). *The wife drought.* Sydney, NSW: Ebury Press.

Dahlen, H., Downe, S., Kennedy, H. P., & Foureur, M. (2014). Is society being reshaped on a microbiological and epigenetic level by the way women give birth?

Midwifery, 30(12), 1149–1151. https://doi.org/10.1016/j.midw.2014.07. 007.

Dahlen, H., Jackson, M., & Stevens, J. (2011). Homebirth, freebirth and doulas: Casualty and consequences of a broken maternity system. *Women and Birth, 24*(1), 47–50. https://doi.org/10.1016/j.wombi.2010.11.002.

Dahlen, H., Kennedy, H. P., Anderson, C. M., Bell, A. F., Clark, A., Foureur, M., … Downe, S. (2013). The EPIIC hypothesis: Intrapartum effects on the neonatal epigenome and consequent health outcomes. *Medical Hypotheses, 80*(5), 656–662. https://doi.org/10.1016/j.mehy.2013.01.017.

Davis-Floyd, R. (2001). The technocratic, humanistic, and holistic paradigms of childbirth. *International Journal of Gynecology & Obstetrics, 75*, S5–S23. https://doi.org/10.1016/S0020-7292(01)00510-0.

Dombroski, K., McKinnon, K., & Healy, S. (2016). Beyond the birth wars: Diverse assemblages of care. *New Zealand Geographer, 72*, 230–239. https://doi.org/10.1111/nzg.12142.

Escobar, A. (2018). *Designs for the pluriverse.* Durham and London: Duke University Press.

Federici, S. (2012). *Revolution at point zero.* Oakland: PM Press.

Feeley, C., & Thomson, G. (2016). Going it alone. *Midwives, 19*(3), 62–65.

Ferguson, J. (2015). *Give a man a fish: Reflections on the new politics of distribution.* Durham: Duke University Press.

Gaskin, I. M. (2011). *Birth matters: A midwife's manifesta.* New York: Seven Stories Press.

Gibson-Graham, J. K. (2006). *A postcapitalist politics.* Minneapolis: University of Minnesota Press.

Gibson-Graham, J. K., Cameron, J., Dombroski, K., Healy, S., Miller, E., & Community Economies Collective. (2017). *Cultivating community economies.* Retrieved February 28, 2019, from TheNextSystem.org website: https://thenextsystem.org/cultivating-community-economies.

Gibson-Graham, J. K., Cameron, J., & Healy, S. (2013). *Take back the economy.* Minneapolis: University of Minnesota Press.

Gudeman, S., & Rivera, A. (1995). From care to house (Del coche a la casa). *American Anthropologist, 97*(2), 242–250.

Jackson, M., Dahlen, H., & Schmied, V. (2012). Birthing outside the system: Perspectives of risk amongst Australian women who have high risk homebirths. *Midwifery, 28*(5), 561–567.

Kitzinger, S. (2006). Birth as rape: There must be an end to 'just in case' obstetrics. *British Journal of Midwifery, 14*(9), 544–545. https://doi.org/10.12968/bjom.2006.14.9.21799.

Latour, B. (2005). *Reassembling the social: An introduction to actor-network-theory.* Oxford and New York: Oxford University Press.

Law, J. (2004). *After method: Mess in social research*. London and New York: Routledge.

MacColl, M.-R. (2009). *The birth wars: The conflict putting Australian women and babies at risk*. St Lucia and Brisbane: University of Queensland Press.

Mol, A. (2008). *The logic of care: Health and the problem of patient choice*. London and New York: Routledge.

Mol, A., & Law, J. (2004). Embodied action, enacted bodies: The example of hypoglycaemia. *Body & Society, 10*(2–3), 43–62. https://doi.org/10.1177/1357034X04042932.

Morrow, O., & Dombroski, K. (2015). Enacting a postcapitalist politics through the sites and practices of life's work. In *Precarious worlds: Contested geographies of social reproduction*. Athens, GA: University of Georgia Press.

OBOS Pregnancy and Birth Contributors. (2014). *Models of maternity care*. Retrieved May 24, 2019, from Our Bodies Ourselves website: https://www.ourbodiesourselves.org/book-excerpts/health-article/models-of-maternity-care/.

O'Brien, M. (1981). *The politics of reproduction*. Boston, London, and Henley: Routledge & Kegan Paul.

Odent, M. (2009). Masculinisation of the birth environment. *Journal of Prenatal and Perinatal Psychology and Health, 23*(3), 185–191.

Paice, E., & Smith, D. (2009). Bullying of trainee doctors is a patient safety issue. *The Clinical Teacher, 6*(1), 13–17. https://doi.org/10.1111/j.1743-498X.2008.00251.x.

Pérez D'Gregorio, R. (2010). Obstetric violence: A new legal term introduced in Venezuela. *International Journal of Gynecology & Obstetrics, 111*(3), 201–202. https://doi.org/10.1016/j.ijgo.2010.09.002.

Reed, R., Sharman, R., & Inglis, C. (2017). Women's descriptions of childbirth trauma relating to care provider actions and interactions. *BMC Pregnancy and Childbirth, 17*(1). https://doi.org/10.1186/s12884-016-1197-0.

Russel, K. (1997). A value-theoretic approach to childbirth. In *Materialist feminism: A reader in class, difference and women's lives* (pp. 328–344). New York and London: Routledge.

Sadler, M., Santos, M. J., Ruiz-Berdún, D., Rojas, G. L., Skoko, E., Gillen, P., & Clausen, J. A. (2016). Moving beyond disrespect and abuse: Addressing the structural dimensions of obstetric violence. *Reproductive Health Matters, 24*(47), 47–55. https://doi.org/10.1016/j.rhm.2016.04.002.

Simpson, M., Schmied, V., Dickson, C., & Dahlen, H. (2018). Postnatal post-traumatic stress: An integrative review. *Women and Birth, 31*(5), 367–379. https://doi.org/10.1016/j.wombi.2017.12.003.

Stephens, J. (2011). *Confronting postmaternalism*. New York: Columbia University Press.

Thornton, C., Schmied, V., Dennis, C.-L., Barnett, B., & Dahlen, H. (2013). *Maternal deaths in NSW (2000–2006) from nonmedical causes (suicide and trauma) in the first year following birth* [Research article]. https://doi.org/10.1155/2013/623743.

World Health Organization. (2018). *WHO recommendations: Intrapartum care for a positive birth experience.* Retrieved from http://www.ncbi.nlm.nih.gov/books/NBK513809/.

CHAPTER 2

Negotiating with Babies

Abstract A healthy baby is the desired outcome of childbirth, but seldom is the agency of the baby given consideration. Seen through the lens of 'choice,' the presence of the foetus and baby is something to be managed. Contradicting this are the daily experiences of pregnancy through which the growing child makes their presence felt. This is so from the first weeks during which a mother may suddenly be no longer in control of her body, and nausea, tiredness or hunger signal a giving over of the body to the work of growing a baby. While the legal personhood of the foetus is much debated, even then, its presence in debate is as a human with a will to live. But in the stories women tell, unborn babies also work to make childbirth unfold. From the start through to the moment of birth (and beyond) mothers and caregivers must work with the baby. In this encounter the relationship is not formed around choice but through an embodied learning characterised by negotiation between the thinking self and the unborn other within.

Keywords Agency · Foetal agency · Baby agency · Embodied learning

At the beginning it was the shock of losing control that really got to me. My body was no longer my own. This was a surprise after spending much of my adult life feeling like I was in charge, pushing my body to do what I wanted it to do: climbing in the mountains, hiking in the back county, training for karate

© The Author(s) 2020
K. McKinnon, *Birthing Work*,
https://doi.org/10.1007/978-981-15-0010-7_2

tournaments. Now suddenly and unexpectedly my body commanded me to stop, to rest, to eat, to sleep RIGHT NOW. I was touring Northland, New Zealand, on the back of a motorbike at the time and was a scant 3 weeks pregnant. I learned very quickly that if I did not attend to my body immediately, 10 minutes later I would be on the verge of falling off the back. The consequences of trying to control my body were immediate, unmistakable. I was no longer in charge. The illusion of being the self I had always been—an individual, self-determining, decision-making, independent being—was irrevocably dissolved. My wellbeing suddenly depended on the needs and rhythms of another—my unborn child.

At the same time, I had to suddenly make a series of changes to how I lived my life. My body demanded frequent food and rest, the leaflets I was given by my midwife informed me that I should be very careful about what I ate: soft cheeses, pre-prepared deli foods, raw eggs or soft yolks, salami, were off the menu. I was instructed to wash salad greens carefully and avoid curly leaf parsley altogether unless it was cooked. Crackers in bed at 5 a.m. to keep away morning sickness, ginger drinks. I couldn't stand to drink coffee anymore, and wine was forbidden. I didn't feel particularly in control of myself or my body, but I carried all the responsibility—the leaflets made me feel like if I did the wrong thing my child would be harmed, and it would be all my fault.

There is much discussion of how the shifts in a woman's body during pregnancy shift her relationship with herself and with people around her. Robyn Longhurst discusses how a pregnant body becomes a kind of public property that can be both sanctioned by others at the same time as a woman's own body may betray her, that suddenly she inhabits a body that may seep or leak (colostrum, waters, urine) (Longhurst, 2000, 2004). At the same time, women can feel proud of their changing bodies, and revel in the new unpredictability of embodied life. These changes in the body, and the changes they elicit in relationships with the self and with others, emerge alongside the development of a new relationship with the growing child within. As these relationships take shape, so too does an emerging sense of oneself as a mother, with attending expectations about what kind of mother you might become, and what kind of birth you might have. These expectations, these new relationships—with yourself, with partners and family, with wider society, and with a baby—accompany women into the birth space. At the same time as a first-time mother might be contending with the emergence of a new kind of self—self-as-mother—she is also experiencing a process of pregnancy and labour that, for many of the women in this study, challenged their sense of control over their bodies.

Scholars of motherhood and mothering have long explored the fraught territory of what it means to become a mother, how it can transform a woman's experiences of being as she negotiates her way through a new set of societal expectations, finds her place in a very personal political debate, and learns to navigate the world in a different body with all the appendages of baby care—prams, nappies, bottles, pacifiers, etc (see, for example, Badruddoja & Motapanyane, 2016; Boyer, 2018; Ruddick, 1989; Stephens, 2011). Beyond the dynamics of identity formation there are also deeper, embodied effects of becoming a mother. Pregnancy changes your brain, and the practice of caring for infants develops habituated behaviours that are not just performed, but embodied (Barha & Galea, 2017; Dombroski, 2018). During pregnancy 'the biological mother's emotional state influences the infant's developing brain,' and even after birth it is the mother who continues to 'act as a regulator of the baby's emotional states' (Schore & McIntosh, 2011). Further, research into the epigenetic impact of childbirth suggests that the way a child is born may have lifelong effects (Dahlen et al., 2013). Altogether, there is compelling evidence that the experience of pregnancy and childbirth sets both mother and baby up for a lifetime. From shaping the foundations for empathy and emotional bonding between mother and child, seeding the health of the baby's microbiome, and supporting a mothers physical and emotional capacity to care, childbirth is seen to have a major impact on what kind of mother a woman is able to become.

Robbie Davis-Floyd argues that not only does the experience of childbirth set up relationships between mother and baby, but that maternity care systems themselves train mothers to take a particular role in the care of their child, and to cede aspects of care responsibilities to the (masculine) authority of medical institutions and the state (see Davis-Floyd, 1993, 2003). I am not convinced that Floyd has the evidence to make quite so strong a claim, but her work provides the important insight that childbirth takes place under powerful social and political structures that shape what it is possible to do, or to be or to think. At the same time, much of the literature advocating for women to have more say in what happens to their bodies seems to forget this. The focus on women being able to make choices about care, including what kind of care they receive, where they give birth, and what happens to their bodies during birth, often seems to assume that women are free to make choices (Dombroski, McKinnon, & Healy, 2016). But freedom is delimited by the social structures we live in, the expectations they set for us, and, as Floyd recognises, the almost instinctive submission

er and authority of medical experts in white coats that we are
d to from early childhood.

ot only are choices never entirely free, the choices we make do not always bring the consequences we expect. And the choices we make during pregnancy and childbirth involve others, such as the unruly pregnant body and the growing child, over whom we do not have control. In this chapter I explore the complexities of decision-making in childbirth, thinking through what it means to make choices in moments when a woman is not free, her body is not cooperative, and there are unspeaking others with whom and for whom decisions must be made—the unborn child chief among them.

TAKING CONTROL AND CEDING CONTROL

Kelly Dombroski, Stephen Healy, and I have explored the implications of positioning pregnant women as 'consumers of healthcare', clients to health care providers with the freedom to choose which provider, and thus which kind of care she will receive. In New Zealand this means choosing a Lead Maternity Carer (LMC) who will be your primary carer, usually a midwife, through pregnancy and childbirth. In Australia this means deciding where you will go for care: your local public hospital, a birth centre, a private obstetrician or an independent midwife. We have argued that these choices can produce considerable anxiety, and in our study it is evident that many women 'progressively discover how little their research and choice matters once they are absorbed into the particular regimes and routines of the place in which birth ends up occurring' (Dombroski et al., 2016, p. 233). While having choices is important, it is also important to recognise that 'the idea that mothers can choose the "best care" for themselves ignores the reality of a fierce political and ideological debate about how a woman should give birth, and leads consumers to assume that a "best choice" is indeed possible' (p. 237). The assumption that there is a right choice to be made is both unreasonable and unfair. We see it as part of larger cultural phenomenon of 'mother blame', that affects women on all sides of the ideological debate about childbirth and parenting. At one extreme, mothers are vilified for being irresponsible and morally suspect for choosing to have a homebirth. At the other extreme, as Chris Bobel recognises, natural mothering literature on attachment parenting, baby-wearing and co-sleeping, engenders guilt and inadequacy for mothers who cannot meet the strict adherence of being 'continually available to their babies' (Bobel, 2004, p. 69). Mothers are made to bear a lot of responsibility, but, as this book articulates, the ways in which labour and childbirth actually unfold are much messier and more complex.

Messiness and complexity were not at the front of Janet's mind as she prepared for her first birth. She prepared herself by learning hypnobirthing, an approach designed to support women through natural birth, letting go of fears and conditioning the release of endorphins using techniques informed by hypnotherapy (Spilsted, 2019). Her first birth did not go smoothly, however, and in the end, she had to undergo an emergency caesarean delivery. The experience was extremely traumatic, and when I interviewed her several years later, even after the much easier delivery of her second child, she remained too traumatised to speak about it, except to relate how she came to completely dismiss the natural birth narrative. For her the idea that the body would just 'know what to do' came to feel like a terrible deception:

> With the first one there was this whole philosophy of hypnobirthing behind it, which went completely terribly wrong. A three to four page birth plan which, in essence, got contradicted in every point that we put in there. [Laughs] So second birth, just cut me open and take the baby out. [Laughs] ...So no spirituality, very practical. No philosophy, no preconceived opinions other than just do it. Just take the baby out. [Laughs]

While Janet spoke about this as a very pragmatic decision, her nervous laughter also conveyed the uncomfortable emotions that continue to affect her. For her second birth, she decided to place her trust 'in the system'. This time she was guided by:

> a belief in Western medicine for a change, which wasn't the same - I didn't have the same opinion when I went into the first birth. But with the second birth, the belief in the power of the Western medical system, and how they can save you from all sorts of difficult situations. So just do what you have to do and trust that you are the professionals, and I give myself into your hands and just take the baby out.

This decision was influenced in part by the desire for '*things to be under control and turn out the way I imagine them*'. Maintaining the sense of being in control was very important, so rather than risk a second emergency caesarean, she chose an elective 'natural caesarean'. The natural caesarean evolved as a technique in response to patient demand and the growing awareness of the need to develop women-centred approaches to surgical delivery (Smith, Plaat, & Fisk, 2008). The technique 'mimics the situation at vaginal birth by allowing (i) the parents to watch the birth of their child as active participants, (ii) slow delivery with physiological autoresuscitation, and (iii) the baby to be transferred directly onto the mother's chest for early skin-to-skin' (Smith et al., 2008, p. 1037). For Janet what was very important was that this technique meant she was immediately able to hold her baby:

> *When they said to me natural caesar I had mixed feelings. Yeah, a natural caesar, right, as if - after having gone through an emergency caesar the first time around. And the second time it was seriously a natural caesar. [Laughs] It's really like that. It is the most natural way that you could possibly have with a caesar.*
>
> *They don't take the baby away from you; it's with you all the time. You're bonding, you're not suffering. You are with the experience all the time. You welcome everything that's happening and it's not like you're dying, it's just all beautiful. It's a necessity to be cut open, to then have the end result, which is a beautiful baby. Then having the baby skin to skin contact, it's almost like giving natural birth.*
>
> *... Like if you give birth naturally, they will still take the baby away, clean the baby, get the baby back to you. It's the same with the caesar. They cut it open, they get it out, clean it, put it back onto you. Very, very natural except for the surgery that's going on. But everything else - the way they handle it is fantastic. Because there are caesarean operations where they don't do that, so that's really well handled.*
>
> *That was important ... It's important that the baby comes out and is only separated for the duration of the cleaning and checking that everything's okay, then immediately back onto you. They did the remaining checks while the baby was still on me, so it was just the bare minimum that the baby was separated from the mother. It's fantastic, it's really good. First baby, we were separated for three hours.*

Between her first and second births, Janet shifted from one philosophy of birth to something very different. Her reasons for doing so are certainly not unusual, as many women who have been through a difficult first birth make radically different decisions about care in later pregnancies. In her case, a first birth that spiralled out of control in distressing ways was healed by finding a way to gain a sense of control in the second. Read in the light of Davis-Floyd's work, this could perhaps be understood as a terrible capitulation to the system, or as a missed opportunity for what Gaskin speaks about as the empowerment and sense of inner strength that comes from childbirth. But for Janet this was the right choice, perhaps the only choice, that could allay her fears of another emergency and ensure that she could see and hold her baby right away.

In contrast, Cath had planned to be at a birth centre for her first baby but was transferred to hospital following concerns that her child was small. In that environment, she was pressured into accepting interventions that she did not feel comfortable with, and berated for wanting to have a more natural birth experience:

> *[The] registrar who had delivered the baby - she was very bossy and not happy with me, with wanting to delay the cord-cutting and all this sort of thing. There were just different issues we had. … I didn't know they were going to have to cut it straightaway. They didn't tell me that until it was right there and then. Of course, you've just had a baby and she was cross with me because my waters broke all over her and I'm like, well oh gosh, you're an obstetrician, aren't you expecting this? When they broke the waters, I don't know, it was just a big rush onto her, I suppose. She got so she was - yeah, anyway. Then when bubs was born - and I didn't really want a forceps delivery, so I was really fighting that - and I suppose she was cross with me for that too. When I say cross, she was actually getting very - I felt - aggressive in her tone of voice to me, saying things about not looking out for the safety of my baby and then things like this.*

For Cath, moving to hospital was what made her sense of control disappear, as she could no longer have what she wanted:

> *I think automatically going into a hospital room like that or a labour ward, that control is to a large extent taken away from you because they've got you on times, they've got you - how labour is progressing according to time.*

Cath was so distressed by her experience in hospital that for her second birth, she chose to give birth at home with no medical support, to 'free-birth'. Cath's experiences are part of a growing trend in Australia, in which women who have experienced trauma and bullying in the hands of obstetricians and midwives, choose to go it alone (Dahlen, Jackson, & Stevens, 2011; Jackson, Dahlen, & Schmied, 2012).

What is particularly insightful about both Janet and Cath's stories are that they highlight the failures of a system in which such stark choices are required. On the one hand, women are assumed to have control over their bodies and the outcomes of their pregnancy and birth—this is what is assumed in the discourses that police pregnant bodies and place the burden of choice on women. On the other hand, women are frequently required to cede all control, whether this occurs consensually and deliberately, as for Janet, or through institutional pressure and bullying, as for Cath. Both experiences can be traumatic, as I will discuss more in later chapters. What I want to focus on here, however, is that choice and control in childbirth are not straightforward. In all cases, from the freebirth experience to the elective caesarean, there are negotiations and compromises.

At a fundamental level no woman in labour is able to make free choices as a singular individual. Any exercise of agency, all choices, occur within constraints. As gender studies scholars Sumi Madhok, Anne Philips, and Kalpana Wilson argue in the introduction to their book '*Gender, Agency and Coercion*' (Madhok, Philips, & Wilson, 2013), these constraints are defined by the ways that our individual autonomy takes shape within our relationships with others. While explorations of agency and choice tend to focus attention primarily on the individual, Madhok et al. argue that agency must be understood to always operate alongside coercion. Agency is 'always exercised within constraints [in which] inequality is an ever-present component, and that constraint relate to social, not just personal, power relations' (p. 7).

The discourses of choice in pregnancy and childbirth fall into the same trap, but there are no free and independent individuals present in pregnancy and birth. The presence of a foetus forces a fundamental shift in how human agency can be understood.[1] Within a mother's body there is another person who is also shaping the process. Julia Kristeva characterised this as the 'dual and alien space' of maternity (Kristeva, 1980; see also Zerilli, 1992). A mother is not just a single individual anymore, but part of a mother–child dyad.

Baby Agency

There are a variety of ways that a mother comes to know the child on the other side of the dyad. Some women feel they know their child well, long before birth. Shamanic midwifery practices that lead a woman through

---

[1] Luce Irigiray and Julia Kristeva are notable Western philosophers who have given serious consideration to what childbearing and mothering mean for individual agency, subjectivity and the 'Otherness' of women in Western thought. Although their contributions are very different, both have opened up debate about what it means to carry a child, as in Kristeva's discussion of the ways that women are thus given to an inherently ethical experience of establishing relationships an 'ethic Other' (Schipper, 2011).

meditation to meet and connect with her unborn child are one example of how a mother and child come to know each other. Interactions between the foetus and others through the wall of the womb is another—several women have shared stories of playing 'footsie' with a baby as he/she stretches out against the inside of the belly. Such examples of a woman's own connection with her unborn child run parallel to more official attention to the mother–child dyad via the information and leaflets that a mother is issued during antenatal care. In these contexts, it is often the child in that dyad who takes a central position, to the extent, at times, of dismissing a mother's concerns altogether.

As Deborah Lupton (2012) demonstrates, much of the information women are routinely given during pregnancy communicate to women the expectation that they must now live and act in the interests of their growing child rather than themselves. This extends to sanctions against smoking or drinking alcohol that may harm the foetus, to dietary restrictions or encouragements to pay more attention to nutrition and exercise. Deborah Lupton's analysis demonstrates how injunctions against certain actions and behaviours, alongside advice on how best to nurture the foetus, vastly overestimate a woman's actual ability to control the 'quality' of the foetus, and often place sole responsibility for foetal health on the mother:

> …this intensity of focus upon pregnant women's actions and the supposed effects on the foetuses they carry serves to unfairly place great pressure upon women to conform to medical and public health advice and positions the foetus' needs as more important than those of the woman. (Lupton, 2012, p. 338)

This trend becomes acutely problematic in cases where women's wishes are ignored, or they are forced to undergo medical procedures based on medical practitioners claiming to act in the best interests of the unborn child. The term 'obstetric violence' is increasingly being used to refer to the intimidation, bullying, coercion, and deliberate physical harm that women are subjected to during childbirth and antenatal and postnatal care. Michelle Sadler et al. (2016) identify that worldwide abuse and disrespect of women during obstetric care is being linked to deeper structural issues of gender inequality. Part of this, it appears, is the tendency to sanction violence against a woman if it is perceived to serve the interests of the unborn child. Thus, an obstetrician who was taken to court in New Jersey for forcing a woman to have a caesarean section, says her actions were justified:

She certainly can refuse the C-section, that is not the problem. I respect patient's opinion. ...[But] I have two patients. I don't have just one patient ...that is why I disagree with the statement of your, of the American, whatever, ACOG [the American Congress of Obstetricians and Gynecologists], that the desire of the mother has to supersede the desire of the foetus. I disagree with that. ...I have an obligation now toward the baby. I've gotta speak for the baby because that is my second patient. (Greenfield, 2015)

As bioethicist Catherine Mills (2014, 2015) recognises, at the heart of 'speaking for the baby' is the question of when does a foetus become a person? The question of whether the foetus is an independent person while still within her mother's body, and whether a foetus needs someone other than the mother to 'speak for' them, has been a core question in many of the debates around abortion and are increasingly of concern in relation to a woman's right to refuse medical procedures during childbirth. Routine ultrasound certainly helps to support the perception of the foetus as already a fully fledged person within (Mills, 2014; Stephenson, McLeod, & Mills, 2016), and the unborn child is already entered into the sociality of life. Images are shared with family and friends, posted on social media. Even the taking of an ultrasound image is a social act: it 'comes into being through an embodied experience and interchange' (Mills, 2014, p. 103) between mother and sonographer, and other witnesses such as the mother's partner, and, of course, the foetus. The foetus is making choices here too, consciously or not: whether to roll to the left or the right, where to position his leg (with the effect of enabling or blocking the view of a stenographer trying to verify his sex). Mills argues that when the ultrasound interacts with legal definitions of personhood, however, the concern is that this could undermine women's reproductive rights at the very same time as enabling reproductive choices in light of diagnosis of foetal abnormalities (2014, p. 103). At what point the interests of the foetus are put before the interests of the mother is a murky question, embedded in the complexities of moral relations, embodiment, and affect. While legal definitions seek to impose clear black-and-white boundaries, in lived experience, mothers and babies have fuzzy edges.

Regret and Responsibility

In the pressure to make the 'right' choice about maternity care, to adhere to the guidelines for certain dietary, exercise, and rest regimes, and to put the child's interests before one's own, women are also made to feel responsible for determining the 'quality' of their baby, and in some cases, are given the responsibility for determining the future health and wellbeing of the child. But there are different ways to think about and take responsibility. For many women in this study the trauma that they carried from their birth experiences came along with disappointment and self-blame for not doing more or making different choices. Jennifer, for example, had a medical condition that meant she was to be admitted to hospital to be monitored from 34 weeks until her baby was born. This intensively medical experience was life-saving and necessary, but also gave rise to (or perhaps exacerbated an existing but undiagnosed) condition of anxiety. As a midwife herself she could see in retrospect that within the parameters of treatment there were different decisions that could have been made and different practices followed to help her become a mother in a less disempowering way. Unlike Janet, whose story told of making a conscious decision to hand herself over to the professionals, Jennifer recalls her own actions as a failure to stand up for herself:

> *They weren't being forceful, but I guess perhaps I was quite passive at the time because I felt, well they know what they're doing, and I don't want to rock the boat and those kinds of things. But definitely if I could I would change quite a lot....*
>
> *I think for me looking back it's very easy to say it was just a series of events that led to that and perhaps if I'd known about the anxiety, if I'd felt more assertive, I would have pushed for things to be quite different. But at the time, for me it was always about doing the right thing. This is what they want us to do, so we'll do that. Don't worry about, you know, just keep doing what they need you to do.*

Davis-Floyd would recognise the desire not to 'rock the boat' as part of our acculturation to the authority of the white-coated professional. This what is called the 'good girl' phenomenon—women wishing to do the 'right' thing and cooperate with the professionals, being polite and nice rather than putting their own needs and wishes first. Sociologist Karin Martin (2003) has argued that this reveals an internalised practice of gender discipline, with women policing themselves to be the good girl. There are also ample stories of doctors seeking to elicit 'good girl' behaviour by telling women their baby is at risk if they do not comply. Jennifer did not experience this, and was never made to feel fearful, but perhaps this is because she did not feel able to push for different things. Among her midwifery colleagues, her sense of sadness about being unable to have a natural birth was not met with sympathy:

> I was quite disappointed with my colleagues. I didn't feel - the one group of women I thought that would have understood why I was disappointed I couldn't have a birth centre birth and experience things the way I wanted, they didn't understand. It was just like well it's always about what's best for the baby. Just have to do what's best for the baby. I'm like, I get that. But can you hear that this is not what I want. I found that again, another reason to keep it all inside because no one understood. There was no one really to talk to about it. I guess I felt safe in the hospital. At least if something happened I just went down to the birthing unit... I guess I acted as if everything was okay. I just kept on going, because we needed to work. I needed the finances. Things like that. So, you just kept going.
>
> But I did love being pregnant. In myself I felt very healthy. I loved that feeling. But just disappointment with the work colleagues that they didn't understand and yet I thought they would have understood that choice is important.

The disappointment and regret carried on well beyond the birth, accentuated by the too-slow emergence of mother-child bond:

> There's a general assumption that as soon as you see your baby there's this wonderful bond. There's this amazing love. Didn't happen for me. Didn't happen until she was at least two. I really - I think that was just another thing as well that was like, what's wrong with me? I don't even - I looked at this baby and I just thought I don't feel anything for you. Probably still off my trolley on drugs, but I just didn't...

Jennifer knows that, having experienced a caesarean under general anaesthetic, and not having the possibility for skin to skin contact and early breastfeeding, all would have impacted on the release of the bonding and attachment hormones (especially oxytocin) that are the biochemical imprints of the 'amazing love' between mother and baby. But this does little to decrease her sense of sadness and ongoing responsibility.

While mothers may feel the ongoing sense of responsibility, of course, it is not only one person in the room making the decisions. At the same time as feeling she 'should have tried harder', Jennifer also allows herself to recognise that perhaps the responsibility does not have to be carried by herself alone:

But part of me also wants to say, well hang on, why was nobody there telling me that there was a way to make it a better experience for both [baby] Max and myself - you know what I mean? Why was my doctor not saying look, we're going to do a C-section, but did you want some skin to skin contact, did you want baby with you in recovery? Instead she went, 'well that went well, and I'll catch you later'.

Truama, disappointment, and regret do not need to be the outcomes of an unexpected turn of events during childbirth. The natural birth that could not happen, the unwanted caesarean, the heavily monitored hospital-bound labour, need not produce such sadness. The majority of women who we interviewed carried at least one experience of great disappointment, and many remained deeply affected by this, years, even decades, afterwards. But there were also many examples of women whose birth plans had gone 'wrong' but whose caregivers had helped them through the process and shared the responsibility with them. Meg, who planned to birth at home but ended up with caesarean deliveries each time, is one such example. Speaking about her midwife, she says:

Because of her I reckon that I've had no hang ups after my c sections at all… You hear about people who really struggle to come to terms with why or they're forced to and things like that, and she had this amazing way of just making sure that all the decisions were joint. So, when I came through, I knew that the path I took was the only option left and the right choice to make and that I owned those decisions. So that I felt that we'd done the right thing for our kids.

Finally, it is not only the mother and her carers that must work together in birth. The baby is an active participant in childbirth in ways that science is only now beginning to understand. While the position of the baby has long been known to affect labour (whether the baby is posterior or breech, and how well the baby has descended into the pelvis, for example) but a more detailed understanding of the role the baby takes in initiating active labour is still the subject of active research. Recent research suggests that it is a chemical signal from the baby that initiates the flood of labour hormones that begin contractions (Gao, Rabbitt, Condon, Renthal, Johnston, & Mitsche, 2015; Gao et al., 2015). During labour the baby also influences how things unfold. Whether the baby is getting stressed by the experience, or is remaining calm, has an important impact on whether the birth will go smoothly. Many mothers talk about the need to work cooperatively with their child during birth, so that the baby may twist and turn as they make their way through the spaces of the mother's pelvis. Some babies even use their feet to leverage themselves out through the birth canal. Here is Cath again, talking about her third birth, which took place at home with the support of a registered independent midwife:

> *When she started to come - when she was actually coming out, she started to push with her feet on my stomach, and I went whoa, and they asked me (like, rather than tell me), they said what's going on Cath? And, I said she's pushing off me, ... I feel that she was in distress and she wasn't getting oxygen. So, she was struggling and then with that in mind I'm thinking I think she needs some help; I pushed really hard to get her out.*

Cath had an instinctive communication with her child. She sensed that her child needed to get out quickly and they both worked to make it happen: the baby pushing and the mother pushing, both together. This is a story of mother and carers *and baby* collaborating together in the work of birth.

CONCLUSION

Becoming a mother involves entering into a co-production of shared existence, a co-becoming, that is felt in the body at the very earliest stages of pregnancy. This chapter has explored how, from the beginning, mothers (and carers and families) have to negotiate a co-becoming *with* the growing foetus. Seen through the lens of 'choice' the presence of the foetus and baby is something to be managed, a passive recipient (and product) of a mothers attentive (or neglectful) care, and the birth itself the result of right (or wrong) decisions made. Contradicting this are the daily experiences of pregnancy through which the growing child makes their presence felt. This is so from the first weeks during which a mother may suddenly be no longer in control of her body, as nausea, tiredness or hunger let her know that the body is given over to the work of growing a baby. Later there are the sensations of a foetus kicking, turning or lodging a knee uncomfortably against a mother's ribcage. The foetus is already its own being, and a range of possibilities exist for forming relationships with the growing child: 'meeting' one's child through meditation or playing inter-utero footsie. Ultrasound scans mean the foetus can already be networked via social media, and ultimately there are laws that determine when a foetus comes into its own personhood. In the stories women tell, unborn babies determine a great deal: positioning themselves to help birth, or to stall it; refusing to come on time, or being in a hurry; being calm and making it easy, or getting stressed; holding still for scan, or not. Babies also do the work of childbirth.

From the start through to the moment of birth (and beyond) mothers and caregivers must work *with* the baby. Thus, from the very beginning, there is an encounter between the agency of a mother making decisions about managing her care, and the inarticulable agency of an unborn child, whose channels of communication are physical, chemical and (for some women) spiritual. In this encounter, the relationship is not formed around choice but through an embodied learning characterised by negotiation between the thinking self and the unborn other within. Maternal work is already, from the very beginning, a collaborative effort between mother and child.

References

Badruddoja, R., & Motapanyane, M. (Eds.). (2016). *"New maternalisms": Tales of motherwork (dislodging the unthinkable)*. Bradford, ON: Demeter Press.

Barha, C. K., & Galea, L. A. M. (2017). The maternal "baby brain" revisited. *Nature Neuroscience, 20*, 134.

Bobel, C. (2004). When good enough isn't: Mother blame in the continuum concept. *Journal of the Association for Research on Mothering, 6*(2), 68–78.

Boyer, K. (2018). *Spaces and politics of motherhood*. London: Rowman & Littlefield.

Dahlen, H., Jackson, M., & Stevens, J. (2011). Homebirth, freebirth and doulas: Casualty and consequences of a broken maternity system. *Women and Birth, 24*(1), 47–50. https://doi.org/10.1016/j.wombi.2010.11.002.

Dahlen, H., Kennedy, H. P., Anderson, C. M., Bell, A. F., Clark, A., Foureur, M., … Downe, S. (2013). The EPIIC hypothesis: Intrapartum effects on the neonatal epigenome and consequent health outcomes. *Medical Hypotheses, 80*(5), 656–662. https://doi.org/10.1016/j.mehy.2013.01.017.

Davis-Floyd, R. (1993). The technocratic model of birth. In *Feminist theory in the study of folklore* (pp. 297–326). Urbana and Champaign: University of Illinois Press.

Davis-Floyd, R. (2003). *Birth as an American rite of passage*. Berkeley: University of California Press.

Dombroski, K. (2018). Learning to be affected: Maternal connection, intuition and "elimination communication". *Emotion, Space and Society, 26*, 72–79. https://doi.org/10.1016/j.emospa.2017.09.004.

Dombroski, K., McKinnon, K., & Healy, S. (2016). Beyond the birth wars: Diverse assemblages of care. *New Zealand Geographer, 72*, 230–239. https://doi.org/10.1111/nzg.12142.

Gao, L., Rabbitt, E. H., Condon, J. C., Renthal, N. E., Johnston, J. M., & Mitsche, M. A. (2015). Molecular mechanisms within fetal lungs initiate labor. *Science Daily*. https://www.sciencedaily.com/releases/2015/06/150622162023.htm.

Gao, L., Rabbitt, E. H., Condon, J. C., Renthal, N. E., Johnston, J. M., Mitsche, M. A., ... Mendelson, C. R. (2015). Steroid receptor coactivators 1 and 2 mediate fetal-to-maternal signaling that initiates parturition. *The Journal of Clinical Investigation, 125*(7), 2808–2824. https://doi.org/10.1172/JCI78544.

Greenfield, B. (2015). *Mom sues doctor over c-section fight: 'I was treated like a child'*. Retrieved from https://www.yahoo.com/news/mom-sues-doctor-over-c-section-fight-i-was-090037592.html.

Jackson, M., Dahlen, H., & Schmied, V. (2012). Birthing outside the system: Perspectives of risk amongst Australian women who have high risk homebirths. *Midwifery, 28*(5), 561–567.

Kristeva, J. (1980). Motherhood according to Giovanni Bellini. In *Desire in language: A semiotic approach to language and literature* (pp. 237–270). New York: Columbia University Press.

Longhurst, R. (2000). 'Corporeographies' of pregnancy: 'Bikini babes'. *Environment and Planning D: Society and Space, 18*(4), 453–472. https://doi.org/10.1068/d234.

Longhurst, R. (2004). *Bodies: Exploring fluid boundaries*. https://doi.org/10.4324/9780203193600.

Lupton, D. (2012). 'Precious cargo': Foetal subjects, risk and reproductive citizenship. *Critical Public Health, 22*(3), 329–340. https://doi.org/10.1080/09581596.2012.657612.

Madhok, S., Philips, A., & Wilson, K. (2013). Introduction. In *Gender, agency and coercion* (pp. 1–13). Basingstoke: Palgrave Macmillan.

Martin, K. A. (2003). Giving birth like a girl. *Gender & Society, 17*(1), 54–72. https://doi.org/10.1177/0891243202238978.

Mills, C. (2014). Making fetal persons: Fetal homicide, ultrasound, and the normative significance of birth. *Philosophia, 4*(1), 88–107.

Mills, C. (2015). The case of the missing hand: Gender, disability, and bodily norms in selective termination. *Hypatia, 30*(1), 82–96.

Ruddick, S. (1989). *Maternal thinking: Towards a politics of peace*. New York: Ballantine Books.

Sadler, M., Santos, M. J., Ruiz-Berdún, D., Rojas, G. L., Skoko, E., Gillen, P., & Clausen, J. A. (2016). Moving beyond disrespect and abuse: Addressing the structural dimensions of obstetric violence. *Reproductive Health Matters, 24*(47), 47–55. https://doi.org/10.1016/j.rhm.2016.04.002.

Schipper, B. (2011). *Julia Kristeva and feminist thought*. Edinburgh: Edinburgh University Press.

Schore, A., & McIntosh, J. (2011). Family law and the neuroscience of attachment. *Family Court Review, 49*(3), 501–512. https://doi.org/10.1111/j.1744-1617.2011.01387.x.

Smith, J., Plaat, F., & Fisk, N. (2008). The natural caesarean: A woman-centred technique. *BJOG: An International Journal of Obstetrics & Gynaecology, 115*(8), 1037–1042. https://doi.org/10.1111/j.1471-0528.2008.01777.x.

Spilsted, M. (2019). *Hypnobirthing Australia*. Retrieved from https://hypnobirthingaustralia.com.au/whatishypnobirthing/.

Stephens, J. (2011). *Confronting postmaternalism*. New York: Columbia University Press.

Stephenson, N., McLeod, K., & Mills, C. (2016). Ambiguous encounters, uncertain foetuses: Women's experiences of obstetric ultrasound. *Feminist Review, 113*(1), 17–33. https://doi.org/10.1057/fr.2016.6.

Zerilli, L. (1992). A process without a subject: Simone de Beauvoir and Julia Kristeva on maternity. *Signs: Journal of Women in Culture and Society, 18*(1), 111–135.

CHAPTER 3

Thinking with Bodies

Abstract The agency of the body is neglected in medical discourses and the expectations embedded in clinical protocols, but it often came up during interviews. In these narratives, the womb is intelligent, the body responsive, the blood carries chemical messages of fear or contentment through the bodies of both mother and child. The body does not (always) respond predictably and carers must respond not only to the will and experience of 'patients' but to the particular and varied configurations of intra-human actors that make up our own bodies. To recognise the thinking body, value the work that it does and permit communion with it, however, requires the displacement of 'rational' thought from its position of privilege, and a space be made for the alter-rationality that belongs to embodied or instinctive thought. A childbirth assemblage encompasses not just a range of actors but a range of associated thought and rationality.

Keywords Instinct · Rationality · Maternal consciousness · Embodiment · Bodily agency · Doctoring

After two days of false starts, my labour finally began in the early hours of the morning. Unable to sleep, I got out of bed and tried to find a comfortable position squatting on a bolster with my head resting on the bed. The midwife came by in the morning, after spending all night supporting another woman through her birth. 'There's a ways to go' she told me and sent me back to bed

© The Author(s) 2020
K. McKinnon, *Birthing Work*,
https://doi.org/10.1007/978-981-15-0010-7_3

to sleep some more. By the early afternoon she was back in the house, and I was in the warmth and support of the birth pool. I was in there for hours while my mother and my partner took turns rubbing my back, and the midwives drank cups of tea and knitted while keeping an eye on me from the living room. The pool was set up in the little sunroom stuck on the side of the house. In between contractions I contemplated our Camellia bush, just outside the window. It was covered in white flowers.

When the urge to push came, everything reached a new level of intensity. The midwives abandoned their cups of tea and rushed in. This baby will be out by sunset, they said, and started bustling about, ready to support me through the second stage of labour. Instead of leaning on the side of the pool, they suggested I lean back on my partner, and with each contraction they encouraged me, push push! But nothing happened. Instead of ramping up, my contractions slowed down. My womb went on strike with my daughter's head halfway down the birth canal—her crown of dark hair could be seen emerging, but everything had stalled. Then came a new round of puzzle solving. They tried to teach me what my body should be doing, moving me forward, moving me back. Push push! Getting me out of the pool and on the toilet, getting me on the bed, pulling on a towel, bracing myself on my legs. Nothing worked. If you reach inside you can feel the head they said, the baby's nearly there! As if comprehending that nearness through my fingertips would get things moving. As if I'd given up and just had to get re-engaged with labour again. I was pushing and didn't know why it wasn't working, what was going wrong? It didn't feel right, but how should it feel? I had never done this before, I thought the body would just know what to do? Finally, one of my midwives fed me some sugar pills, and they put me on a drip. I was pushing so hard that I was forcing my own blood back up through the tubing.

We were all trying to speak to my body—push push! But that baby wasn't moving. At last they decided I needed to go to hospital. Up off the bed I got and two steps towards the front door was overtaken by a massive contraction: this is what it ought to have been feeling like. Two more steps and we had to pause again, each time the contractions were stronger than they had been for hours. Everyone around me was still saying 'push push!' But I didn't need to try to push, my body was doing all the work on its own. About 45 minutes later, my daughter was born.

In childbirth, not only must the mother (and the baby, and their carers) work, but her body must do work also. The work of the body must traverse both senses of the verb: the body must 'work' as in 'function' properly or effectively; and the body must also 'do work' as in effortful activity in order to achieve a result (Oxford English Dictionary, 2019). When the body is not working as it should, how do you remind it of the task at hand? How do you tell a body what to do when it is suddenly unresponsive? French philosopher Jean-Luc Nancy and geographer Mitch Rose (while neither have ever given birth themselves) provide some thought-provoking language for thinking through this dilemma, and in doing so strive to articulate the complex relationships between our conscious selves and the working body. Nancy reflects on his experience of a heart attack during which his heart revealed itself no longer just 'part of him, an intimate component of his being' but 'an intruder, something foreign and utterly outside his dominion' (Rose, 2018, p. 1127). The heart (and by extension the womb), are in Mitch Rose's words 'material agencies' that are both elements of existence and things 'outside us', 'things that have a life of their own, unaccountable to us or the urgency of our reliance'. For Rose, and for Nancy, the material agency of the body is alien because it is unresponsive to and exists outside our conscious self. I would put it differently: these things are parts of us, parts of our body, that sustain and give life, but they have their own agency. The point is that we do not have dominion over our own bodies; the body, the heart, the womb, have their own will.

The agency of the body may deny us full possession of the self, but it does not mean that the body is not also, at the same time, part of ourselves—daily life is a constant to-and-fro between our bodily existence and our conscious activity. As Robyn Longhurst's work on the maternal body shows, these negotiations take place in, and transform our relationships with, places and spaces (2012). And they transform our relationships with ourselves. In the example of a heart attack, or many illnesses, the body makes itself suddenly present in a new and different way—by the heart malfunctioning suddenly we feel its presence (we are 'touched' by it, as Nancy says, in a different way) and recognise it suddenly as an alien, an 'intruder'. In childbirth, the body is also doing its own thing but, unlike in a heart attack, mothers, caregivers and support people are doing more than just responding to a life-giving function suddenly going wrong. We are instead trying to communicate with it, to help it along, to *work with it* (push push!). In this, our relations with the workings of the body during childbirth are more akin to other chronic bodily workings: the daily negotiations with blood sugar for the diabetic, the management of intermittent migraines, or the monthly encounters with blood, bloating, and pain that accompany the menstrual cycle. These things do not 'just happen', but are managed, responded to, negotiated with. The same goes for the workings of the body during childbirth.

Women and caregivers talk about efforts to manage and communicate with the birthing body in a range of ways, and in this chapter, I explore how these communications rest upon particular forms of consciousness. I experiment with Rose's idea that consciousness is in essence about self-awareness, and in turn (an attempt at) self-possession. Sometimes consciousness, and the conscious communications and actions taken during childbirth, can be seen as attempts at self-possession. But often it is something else. Something that is less about mastery, something that is felt more than articulated. Something that could perhaps, following Sarah Ruddick, be described as a 'maternal consciousness'—in between thought and feeling, something other than rationality or will, found somewhere in the efforts to commune with the birthing body.

Instinct and the Animal Self

The part of human experience that is beyond consciousness, that is felt rather than articulated (the part that belongs to what Underhill-Sem calls 'pinchable bodies', 2001), is not quite will or rational thought, is often characterised as 'instinctive'. Discussions about instinct have in the past linked humans to the animal part of ourselves. The fight or flight response is embedded in the 'reptilian' part of our brain, the seat of the limbic system, located just above the brainstem (Lewis, Amini, & Lannon, 2001); uncontrolled human aggression is called 'animal'. The instinct of the body in childbirth is evoked in the idea that the body 'knows' what to do. This 'knowing' sits at the centre of the debate between natural birth advocates, who trust that most of the time, the body knows what to do, and advocates of a risk-averse medical-technocratic model, who do not. For many on the medical side, the body needs to be carefully controlled and managed through the birth process.

Ina May Gaskin's lifelong work as a midwife and natural birth activist and educator has been to affirm that women's bodies, no matter what part of the world they are from, are well equipped to give birth to babies. Gaskin repeatedly makes the point that:

> Special interventions in the birth process should be no more necessary among human females that they are among other female mammals, as long as we humans are well nourished, fit, aware of how our bodies and minds work, and

healthy. I repeat, we humans are not inferior to hamsters, rhinoceri, squir-rels, or aardvarks in our reproductive design. It's our minds that sometimes complicate things for us. (Gaskin, 2011, p. 23)

Reflecting on her midwifery experience, Gaskin suggests that complications of the mind are often a problem among women who are intelligent, 'often competitive' and who 'by force of habit, would try to "think" their babies out' (p. 37):

> I often found it easier to take the shortcut of explaining to women that we all have an inner primate, and that this is the part of ourselves that we need to access when we are in labour. 'Let your monkey do it' became the phrase I used to say to those [women]…it seems to help them is they understand that optimum labour requires them to enter into a trance state – not a logical thinking state. (p. 37)

In contrast to Gaskin's writings, which often refer readers to the examples of animal or mammalian examples of labour and of touch, the likening of a woman's experience to an animal's experience is not always so positive. One of the obstetricians we spoke with was also fond of animal metaphors but used them differently—usually to raise questions about a woman's desires. Michael, a GP-obstetrician from New Zealand, found it difficult to accept that a woman ought to give birth while standing or on hands and knees:

> …I don't much like hands and knees. I find it a difficult position to assess people in. Also, there's always poos around when babies are born. If you're on your knees, then the poos slide out of your bottom, all over your vulva and all over the top of the baby's head. You've got a constant cleaning job to do. It just doesn't seem to be a sensible way to do it. Even sheep don't do it standing up. They lie down, or lie on their side.

In this case, the obstetrician's preference for women to lie on a bed is more about what is easier for him as he assesses the progress of the birth and helps to deliver a baby. But the punchline is about *not even sheep* do it standing up, as if a woman who insists on standing rather than lying down might have lost touch with what an animal might consider sensible, as if a woman who stands might be considered even less intelligent in birth than a sheep.

This attitude is rather shocking to many contemporary birth profession-als, who are well aware of the significant body of research that demonstrates that when women are able to move into the position they prefer, it helps to support the movement of the baby through the pelvis, making more space and increasing the likelihood of normal vaginal delivery. The World Health Organization's guidelines on intrapartum care state specifically that women should have the freedom to move around during the early stages of labour and to choose their position for birth (World Health Organization, 2018). These 'choices' are not usually made in an informed and conscious way, but in response to the imperatives issued by a body in labour. When a woman is in the midst of labour, and responding to those bodily imperatives, it is her 'monkey' that is doing it.

To a trained and responsive ear, the raw animalistic cry of a woman in labour will tell what stage the labour is at. It is the monkey-self speaking through that cry, but as Gaskin suggests, and as many of our respondents agreed, it is not easy to shift into that state. Midwife Melanie made it clear:

> It's hard work. It's called labour. It's hard work and it's painful and it's also a really altered state and if you are not prepared for that it's so - I can now see how it is so easy to be flipped out by it. I think a lot of women just flip out.

This altered state and the experience of 'flipping out' is perhaps what many women struggled to find words for as they told us their birth stories. We heard this in the tendency to describe the rawness and power of the experience of birth. Women who had experienced a natural labour and birth often spoke about being mentally and emotionally in a state in which 'rational' thought and expression were not possible: they were 'in the zone', in 'labour land', or just unable to speak. This state is somewhere akin to meditation, a concentrated turning inwards, a place where language fails.

A Maternal Consciousness?

It is not easy to speak about the state of being in 'the zone'. The language available to speak about a state of mind in which rational thought or careful speech are difficult tend to be dismissive: women in this state are 'irrational', or 'emotional', (or 'flipped out'). Is there another way to speak about this state of being? Mitch Rose argues that consciousness is 'a gesture of self-possession' (p. 1129). It is an attempt to claim oneself in the face of a precarious and enigmatic world. Consciousness, he says, is a 'desperate and grasping' attempt to 'pull oneself together; as an attempt to master a world that interminably eludes us' (Rose, 2018, p. 1132). I wonder if, in labour land, what is required is a shift to a different kind of consciousness.

One that is not even attempting the task of making sense of what is going on, or to represent it, pull meaning from it, or to place the ego in relation to it.

While Gaskin offers the monkey as one way to speak about this altered consciousness, for me, this analogy sits too close to the long history of misogynist Western philosophy that positioned women as slightly less human than men, an 'other' or 'second sex' (ref) to a norm defined around the masculine (de Beauvoir, 1952). Women were meant to be 'naturally' inclined towards love and care. Women were 'emotional' or 'irrational' and as a result, were not capable of leadership, governing, or contribution in meaningful ways to the 'high' pursuits of intellectual debate, art-making, or poetry. These heights of human achievement were linked to something Sara Ruddick represents as a masculine form of Reason, a mode of thought that was thought to have no relationship to emotion or instinct (Ruddick, 1989). These days we know better, and an ever-increasing body of literature is providing an understanding of the physiology of emotion, demonstrating how emotions play a crucial part in education, brain development, intelligence, regulation of attention, pain, and effective rational decision-making processes (Davidson & Sutton, 1995; Lerner, Li, Valdesolo, & Kassam, 2015; Lewis et al., 2001; Slovic, Finucane, Peters, & MacGregor, 2004; Wielgosz, Goldberg, Kral, Dunne, & Davidson, 2019). There is also an increasing recognition of 'emotional labour' as a form of work, paid or unpaid, that requires loving care: Arlie Hochschild coined the term in relation to flight attendants (Hochschild, 2003), but the term is now used to talk about the loving care required in all kinds of work contexts, including the work of child-rearing.

Ruddick offers us a different way to perceive reason and rational thought, and to comprehend and value the knowledge and insight that comes from the maternal experience. For her, the work of bearing children, nurturing them, caring for them (whether as a male or female parent) gives rise to a different kind of intellect and a different kind of rationality linked to something she calls 'maternal thought'—the thinking through that is required when a person is engaged with the practice of maternal work, of preserving a child's life, nurturing her emotional and intellectual growth, and training her into social acceptability. Ruddick's revolutionary proposal is that this work requires deep intellectual struggle, problem-solving, and moral and ethical reflection in the midst of and channelled through (an often passionate) love—accompanied inevitably also by anger, pain, disappointment, and failure. Maternal care is not always nice or just. The key point, however, is that it is still *thought*: Ruddick argues that maternal thinking involves as much careful consideration and training of mind and habit as rational thought, for all that it is also about care and love.

Such considered habits and practices are also embodied—they are felt, learned, practised, and remembered in and through bodies. Kelly Dombroski makes this clear in her research on maternal connection, intuition and the practice of 'elimination communication' (EC), a form of infant toileting that minimises nappy use (Dombroski, 2018). Practising EC requires carers to learn to be affected by infant communication, becoming responsive to non-verbal cues of an infant's need to urinate or defecate. Dombroski's study describes the way that this practice develops an embodied connection between carer and child, a *learned intuition*.

Ruddick's work on the thinking involved in maternal love and care, and Dombroski's work on the learning of an embodied maternal intuition, offer an opportunity to reposition Gaskin's 'monkey self' not as animal, but as a self that is expert in a different kind of rationality, whose mode of communication is not verbal but sensory. In the distant terrain of 'labour land', something that is neither just of the body, nor just of the speaking, decision-making self, comes into play. That altered state makes possible a 'maternal consciousness' particular to the shared body-mind work of labour.

THE DARK SPACES OF LABOUR LAND

Although entering this state of maternal consciousness and travelling to 'the zone' featured in many birth stories, what also featured was the frequency with which that zone was difficult to reach, and the body was not always willing to cooperate. Despite all this talk of the instinctive, mammalian female body, the body doesn't always just 'know what to do'. Sometimes the cervix simply does not want to stretch. The womb simply does not want to contract. Sometimes the heart and lungs are not up to the hard work of labour. Sometimes the blood does not spread the right hormones around at the right time, or coagulate when it is meant to, or, the placenta gets stuck to the womb. Bodies do not always work as they are supposed to, and the job of the caregiver is to watch and test and predict, to respond when the body cannot.

A big part of this watchfulness is the work of coaxing the body to do what it needs to do. Many midwives 'speak' back to the body, to the primate-self, by using quiet, darkness, and calming touch. For many midwives this means keeping women in a space where they were comfortable, where they felt safe and supported, whether this was at home or in a hospital. For midwife Sally, a New Zealand midwife who supported women to birth both in hospitals and at home, the most important thing was to ensure a woman was in a space of comfort:

> *It's a quiet space. It's usually a dark space... It's usually soft. Having said that, a lot of the time it's the bathroom. It's a space where women feel comfortable... Generally, I find women are in a place in themselves where their face is covered. So, whether they've got their face in a pillow or their face in the corner of the shower or wherever it is, they generally will hide their face. Then you've got the water births and if they're not in an all fours position with their face hidden, they don't want to see they're looking at you. Even then they'll close their eyes. I think it takes a lot of concentration to have a baby.*

The space itself becomes a tool for communication, a way of telling the woman that things are ok, providing an environment in which she can remain in a state of concentration. This also means recognising that verbal communication, rational thought, and calculation should be allowed to become secondary, allowing the 'animal' self, seated in the limbic brain, to come to the fore. Sally spoke a lot about the importance of the dark and private 'cave' in which a woman could feel safe enough to retreat into 'labour land':

> *... the way birthing is at the moment in hospitals and stuff, I'm surprised that women actually birth. All the stuff we know about the limbic system and relaxing and dark and quiet and all those things so you can get out of your thinking brain. How do women birth in bright lights and 10 people in the room? I guess they have forceps and they're pulled out of them.*
>
> *That environment is really important, and I think that covering your face is part of that going into your dark cave where you feel safe. So, if you can't create a cave in the lounge room at home or in your bedroom or whatever, you do that in the hospital room or in the hospital bathroom or whatever, the birth centre. So they - that little space just becomes them.*
>
> *If they're constantly interrupted and asked questions, even the simple questions, do you want a drink? You have to be pulled out of that system to think well, do I want a drink, am I thirsty, and find that answer. We all know that when you look at a labouring woman, her eyes are rolling around in her head with the endorphins that are flowing, if she's left alone to feel safe and hasn't had any artificial induction or medications.*

Sally spoke about how many women will choose a space that is small and dark, even if they have envisioned giving birth in a very different space with light and views. She alluded to the deeply embedded fight or flight response which, in prehistoric times, would have presumably led a woman to birth in the safety of a cave rather than out in the open where the sabre tooth tiger might attack:

> *I see that all the time. I had another woman recently who put her birth pool in the bay window, which overlooked the bay and it was just beautiful... The bathroom was on the opposite side of the house and had plantation shutters which were closed. It was dark in there. That's where she birthed. She went in there to go to the bathroom and never really came out. I said did you want to go to the pool? No. Of course she didn't. Way too bright, too many tigers there.*

The dark spaces and the quiet are what speak to a woman's 'inner primate', along with touch. This is something that Ina May Gaskin describes as 'conscious touch', and is elsewhere termed 'therapeutic touch'—touch is a way of communicating also. As anthropologist Sheila Kitzinger discusses,

> [A midwife] receives information through the sensitivity of her touch, and gives comfort, confidence and courage by touch. A good midwife knows exactly how and when to touch, just as she also knows when to be hands off. (Kitzinger, 2011)

The recognition that darkness, quiet, and not being engaged with verbally, was important in supporting birth, was recognised not just by midwives but also by obstetricians we spoke to. Michael, for example, an obstetrician in a New Zealand hospital, said:

> *What you've got to remember is it's a natural process going on. If there's no engagement required because the process is going well, let's not interfere. If they're resting well between contractions, why would we interrupt them and say - start talking about something that they don't need to talk about. So, everybody's different, and like any consultation, it follows the course it needs to follow. That's more driven by the woman than by us.*

Both Michael and Sally are recognising and practising the protection of what Sarah Buckley talks about as 'undisturbed birth' (Buckley, 2005, 2015). Undisturbed birth is an approach that seeks to, as much as possible, create a space of protection around a mother in labour so as to best support the hormonal physiology of birth. It is based on evidence that maintaining an optimal balance of the hormones released during labour, maximising the natural release of oxytocin, for example, and seeking minimal release of stress hormones, supports effective natural labour and delivery—'physiological childbirth':

> Consistent and coherent evidence finds that physiologic childbearing facilitates beneficial (salutogenic) outcomes in women and babies by promoting foetal readiness for birth and safety during labour, enhancing labour effectiveness, providing physiologic help with labour stress and pain, promoting maternal and newborn transitions and maternal adaptations, and optimizing breastfeeding and maternal-infant attachment. (Buckley, 2015, p. x)

By protecting undisturbed birth, caregivers are communicating to a woman's birthing self, her animal self, a self that does not speak so much as sense and feel. That sensing and feeling might take place *by* a woman and *in* a woman, but usually it unfolds distinct from conscious will. The exhortation to 'push push' reaches a conscious mind, but not the sensing-feeling body-self that Gaskin calls the inner-primate, and I have suggested might be termed a maternal consciousness. Dark and quiet spaces, gentle touch, help that self to emerge, but it is not so easy to coerce the body-self—it has a mind of its own.

THE INTELLIGENT BODY

The idea that the body has an agency of its own is increasingly being explored in the texts of social researchers such as Annemarie Mol (2002, 2008) or Bruno Latour (2004), and in journals such as *Body and Society*. Mol's work, explores the way that medical conditions such as diabetes become understood and acted upon through collaborative efforts of patients and doctors (discussed further in Chapter 5) alongside technologies and instruments, blood and bodies. The body, in her account, cannot be subjugated—it does not cooperate. Thus diabetes care must be *attentive* to fragile bodies, adjusting and responding: 'We do not engage in care despite, but with, our bodies' (Mol, 2008, p. 45). Rachel Colls and Maria Fannin (2013) take their attention a step further, to consider not only how we must relate to bodies, but how bodies relate within themselves, exploring the placenta as an organ that can teach us about the relationality of interior bodily surfaces. The body is a 'lively' thing, an 'agential object' as

Colls and Fannin put it (p. 1100) that we can think *with*, and in doing so reveal something of the relations between bodies and subjects. Accounts of childbirth from midwives and obstetricians we interviewed also highlighted how the body is something to work *with*, but also how important it is to step back and let the body take over.

The birthing body is an intelligent body, as noted by New Zealand obstetrician, Peter. An unlikely source for such musings, in the rest of my conversation with Peter he was positioning himself very clearly as an advocate for a medical view of birth. He could not understand why any woman would just trust that the body 'knew what to do', and not ensure she was close to medical assistance should it be needed. Yet, he also spoke of the body as a knowing thing:

> *I think, on a personal note, I'm constantly surprised by the ability of the body to do what it needs to do. I think often a good example of that is if you are perhaps repairing a perineal tear and being very aware of Mum's hormonal response to Baby, even though Baby's on the other side of the room with the uterine contractions obviously from oxytocins release to Baby whose yelling demands from across the other side of the room. They don't even know what they're doing yet, but your body's clearly doing the right things.*

> *Facilitator: Responding already.*

> *Responding, yeah. In fact, that - an example the other day of a [multi] para 5 came in with an undiagnosed transverse lie, ruptured membranes, prolapsed [arm] ... and her uterus had stopped contracting, which was very useful, but probably very intelligent as well. It's not the first time I've seen that where there's a good time in which the uterus needs to stop contracting and it does because it kind of knows what it's doing.*

When given the freedom to speak on a 'personal note,' Peter is able to acknowledge that a uterus can 'know what it's doing': it responds to a baby's cries, it stops contracting when it ought to, it is intelligent. These are not acknowledgements that sit easily with dominant biomedical understandings of the body as a system or 'machine' (Davis & Walker, 2010).

The body that 'knows' is also a body that acts. In childbirth, in the 'altered state' of labour land, the body is acting beyond any conscious control—as evidenced by the feeling of being overwhelmed or out of control that so many of our respondents, mothers, midwives and doctors alike, spoke about. Grace gave birth in a Sydney hospital, and articulates well the feeling of being out of control and needing help to learn how to work with the body in a different way:

> *I was yelling and making a hell of a noise. I don't know if it's more painful if it's a quick birth or whatever I don't know. But it seemed very suddenly intense. There didn't seem to be much build up to it. So instantly the gas was just available and I just dragged on it as a kind of lifeline thing, something to do. But when I was pushing, my midwife said at one point, Why do you think you need the gas? I said, I'm afraid. She said, What are you afraid of? I said, Of the pain. She said, Well what I want you to do is try breathing in a particular way. She helped me to do that and then I stopped using the gas for the last bit. I don't remember how much.*
>
> *I think it was quite frightening. The physical pain and the physical nature of it was, I found, quite frightening. I remember in the antenatal classes they talk to you about the transition period and it sounded like this horrible phase, that it was the thing that I was afraid of. I wasn't really afraid of anything else, but I was afraid of being out of control. They said it was a feeling of being out of control. It felt like quite a lot of the labour felt like that. Like just this sudden very severe pain and hardly time to draw breath between the next one. Not wanting the next one to come but not having any choice that it's coming. Once I got into the pushing and into the rhythm of the pushing that felt better. I was very tired by that stage.*
>
> *I remember my limbs shaking, especially when the head had come out - oh I think her body had come out and then they said, you know, you have to push the placenta. You're just like - you've got to be kidding [laughs]. I remember my legs completely wobbling and shaking like that as I was trying to stand up and push the placenta out. Then we went home the next day.*

When labour does go well, it is a moment when the body takes over, and for many women this take-over is experienced as shocking and difficult. For many women it is confronting to lose hold of self-possession and will, to discover that the body can have such a strong will of its own.

ABANDONING MASTERY OVER THE BODY

The maternity care systems in which my interviewees received antenatal care did not ready them for the experience of discovering a wilful body. In contrast, much antenatal education instead teaches women to trust the knowledge of medical practitioners over their self-knowledge. K. K. Barker (1998) took a look at the pregnancy information leaflets produced by the US government in the early twentieth century to unravel part of the slow journey through which women became no longer the experts in their own bodies. These leaflets, produced in the 1920s and 1930s, span the decades in which women were first encouraged to see their doctors throughout pregnancy. Antenatal care is now normalised, but at that time women did not go to their doctors unless they knew something was going wrong with the pregnancy. Within a decade of the first pamphlet produced in 1924, recommendations for Prenatal care by the United States Children's Bureau:

> moves sharply away from the focus on what women could do for themselves to ensure their safety and the safety of their children to the elemental need to defer to a physician. There is a shift away from hygiene to a focus on medical supervision; a shift away from preventive remedies to a focus on medical therapeutics; and an increasing emphasis on the need to monitor all pregnancies using technology. (Barker, 1998, p. 1073)

One of the key shifts that Barker identified was that, prior to this time, it was normal for women themselves to hold the knowledge of how to care for themselves through pregnancy, and how it felt when things were not right. What Barker charts is the introduction of a new norm, in which it was the doctors, and only the doctors, who held legitimate knowledge about pregnancy and birth. She argues that what was going on was a 'delegitimation of non-scientific knowledge about pregnancy' that entailed 'a shift in who is seen as expert' (p. 1071). Women stopped being the experts of their own bodies, handing that authoritative knowledge over to medical experts (a movement also discussed at length by the contributors to Davis-Floyd & Sargent, 1997).

Conclusion: Thinking Bodies

Thinking is not only done in bodies, it is done by bodies. The biophysical processes of birth are supposed to respond in predictable ways to specific interventions. The experience of birthing women and their carers tells a different story. In these narratives, the womb is intelligent, the body responsive, the blood carries chemical messages of fear or contentment through the bodies of both mother and child. For many participants in the study, the unseen, but often strongly felt, bodily actors in the birth space highlighted the importance of internal communion during labour. For carers, it also signalled the need to work with the myriad of autonomous actors that make up our selves, seeking ways not just to measure and test for what is going on in the blood or urine, but to create spaces that spoke to these animal selves. Spaces of quiet, of darkness, spaces of safety and of letting go, spaces where the thinking of the body might take precedence over the thinking of a woman. To recognise the thinking body, value the work that it does and permit communion with it, however, requires the displacement of 'rational' thought from its position of privilege and a space to be made for the alter-rationality that belongs to embodied or instinctive thought.

The conscious self, the self-possessing self, has to step aside and rather than seeking what Rose identifies as 'mastery', must seek to work with that animal self instead, allowing a maternal consciousness to take over. The way Grace was helped to breathe through her pain, the dark quiet spaces and protection that caregivers provide, the space that allows a woman to turn inward—these are the conduits to communication with Gaskin's monkey-self and the intelligent womb of Peter's account. These are ways to work alongside a body that contains its own agency that may or may not be responsive to the ways in which we try to coax and communicate with it. Recognition of a childbirth assemblage requires then, not just a range of actors, but different associated consciousness, embedded somewhere in the sensing-feeling body.

References

Barker, K. K. (1998). A ship upon a stormy sea: The medicalization of pregnancy. *Social Science & Medicine, 47*(8), 1067–1076. https://doi.org/10.1016/S0277-9536(98)00155-5.

Buckley, S. J. (2005). *Gentle birth, gentle mothering.* Brisbane: One Moon Press.

Buckley, S. J. (2015). *Hormonal physiology of childbearing: Evidence and implications for women, babies, and maternity care.* Washington, DC: Childbirth Connection Programs, National Partnership for Women & Families.

Colls, R., & Fannin, M. (2013). Placental surfaces and the geographies of bodily interiors. *Environment and Planning A, 45,* 1087–1104.

Davidson, R. J., & Sutton, S. K. (1995). Affective neuroscience: The emergence of a discipline. *Current Opinion in Neurobiology, 5*(2), 217–224. https://doi.org/10.1016/0959-4388(95)80029-8.

Davis, D. L., & Walker, K. (2010). Re-discovering the material body in midwifery through an exploration of theories of embodiment. *Midwifery, 26*(4), 457–462. https://doi.org/10.1016/j.midw.2008.10.004.

Davis-Floyd, R., & Sargent, C. (1997). *Childbirth and authoritative knowledge: Cross-cultural perspectives.* Berkeley: University of California Press.

de Beauvoir, S. (1952). *The second sex.* New York: Knopf.

Dombroski, K. (2018). Learning to be affected: Maternal connection, intuition and "elimination communication." *Emotion, Space and Society, 26,* 72–79. https://doi.org/10.1016/j.emospa.2017.09.004.

Gaskin, I. M. (2011). *Birth matters: A midwife's manifesta.* New York: Seven Stories Press.

Hochschild, A. R. (2003). *The managed heart: Commercialization of human feeling* (20th anniversary ed.). Berkeley, CA: University of California Press.

Kitzinger, S. (2011). *Rediscovering birth.* London: Pinter and Martin Publishers.

Latour, B. (2004). How to talk about the body? The normative dimension of science studies. *Body & Society, 10*(2–3), 205–229. https://doi.org/10.1177/1357034X04042943.

Lerner, J. S., Li, Y., Valdesolo, P., & Kassam, K. S. (2015). Emotion and decision making. *Annual Review of Psychology, 66*(1), 799–823. https://doi.org/10.1146/annurev-psych-010213-115043.

Lewis, T., Amini, F., & Lannon, R. (2001). *A general theory of love.* New York: Vintage.

Longhurst, Robyn. (2012). *Maternities: Gender, Bodies and Space.* London and New York: Routledge.

Mol, A. (2002). *The body multiple: Ontology in medical practice.* Durham: Duke University Press.

Mol, A. (2008). *The logic of care: Health and the problem of patient choice.* London and New York: Routledge.

Oxford English Dictionary. (2019). *Work.* Retrieved from Oxford Living Dictionaries—English website: https://en.oxforddictionaries.com/definition/work.

Rose, M. (2018). Consciousness as claiming: Practice and habit in an enigmatic world. *Environment and Planning D: Society and Space, 36*(6), 1120–1135. https://doi.org/10.1177/0263775818784754.

Ruddick, S. (1989). *Maternal thinking: Towards a politics of peace.* New York: Ballantine Books.

Slovic, P., Finucane, M. L., Peters, E., & MacGregor, D. G. (2004). Risk as analysis and risk as feelings: Some thoughts about affect, reason, risk, and rationality. *Risk Analysis, 24*(2), 311–322. https://doi.org/10.1111/j.0272-4332.2004.00433.x.

Underhill-Sem, Y. (2001). Maternities in 'out-of-the-way' places: Epistemological possibilities for retheorising population geography. *International Journal of Population Geography, 7*(6), 447–460. https://doi.org/10.1002/ijpg.241.

Wielgosz, J., Goldberg, S. B., Kral, T. R. A., Dunne, J. D., & Davidson, R. J. (2019). Mindfulness meditation and psychopathology. *Annual Review of Clinical Psychology, 15*(1). https://doi.org/10.1146/annurev-clinpsy-021815-093423.

World Health Organization. (2018). *WHO recommendations: Intrapartum care for a positive birth experience.* Retrieved from http://www.ncbi.nlm.nih.gov/books/NBK513809/.

CHAPTER 4

Becoming Mothers Alongside a Roomful of Things

Abstract This chapter takes the example of the bed to explore the ways in which the relationships between humans and objects within the birth space position both as actors that produce (un)certain outcomes. The bed is caught up in a set of productive relationships, sharing a role in the birth space with the decision-making, thinking woman. Sitting in the centre of most birth wards, the bed calls a woman to lie down upon it, and this call may be welcomed or it may be resisted, the bed may support a woman or it may become an obstruction, even a prison. Thinking with Heidegger's ruminations on the 'thingness of things' I argue that the 'bedness of the bed' shows us both the way an object is its own entity (made by us, given purpose by its use, with its own presence) while moving us in particular ways—this inanimate thing in the room produces human action. To be attentive to the agency of the bed itself and the way it is caught up in complex relationships (with tangible effects on the experience of birth), highlights the way that the conscious self must encounter an excess of decisions with consequences that are not always obvious.

Keywords Things · Thingness · Agentic objects · Non-human

The bed rules the room. Heavy, immoveable, my bed at home is a nest of comfort, crumpled blankets and soft pillows smelling softly of sleep. For me, the bed is home for the weeks following birth, a little hollow to hide in and snuggle

© The Author(s) 2020
K. McKinnon, *Birthing Work*,
https://doi.org/10.1007/978-981-15-0010-7_4

and get to know each other. Propped up on cushions, working hard to perfect the art of breastfeeding—re-learning with each child who brings a new and different approach. Nappy change station set up on the foot of the bed. All the necessary paraphernalia scattered close to hand—the bottomless cups of herbal tea, hot packs for the back, frozen cabbage leaves for the swollen breasts, paracetamol for the after-birth pains that get worse with every child, piles of nappies, restorative concoctions of 'tigers milk' to aid my body knit back together and feed the milk production, ready stacks of towels to catch the baby spills. The day passes in 3–4 hour blocks of feeding, burping, peeing, pooing, swaddling, and rockrockrocking back to sleep, in the endless twilight of a fuzzy brain, all centred on this hulking creature at the centre of the room – the gentle giant that cradles us as we rest. The bed is where this baby was conceived, in the dark, or perhaps a stolen afternoon in the half light of curtains drawn. The bed is where I laboured through a long night, the sturdy frame offering reassurance.

The bed at the centre of the hospital room is a different thing. It is crisp and clean, tight corners, sharp edges. This bed is not a place for gentle comfort, it is not wide enough for cuddles. It was the stinginess of the bed that drove me to my first homebirth—I could not contemplate spending my first night as a mother in such a lonely repose, no room for our newly expanded family to hold each other and be held through the first night of this new life. When I found myself unexpectedly on that hospital bed, it proved itself a gogogadget bed: it goes up, it goes down, there are side rails to hold onto, and pieces that detach to allow everyone to get a better look, and on each side, epoxy-coated high-quality steel lithotomy rods allowed my feet to be elevated and strapped into 'stirrups'. (The bed got me into what one obstetrician in the research called the 'stranded beetle position'). It felt neither comforting nor reassuring.

The bed, an object central to so many births around the world, does not sit neutral and disengaged in the birthing room. The bed's presence in the birth space *does* something, it shapes that space in particular ways, which in turn, shape a woman's experience of birth. This chapter is an account of some of those particularities.

In this book so far, I have discussed some of the ways in which a woman in labour must contend with multiple demands as she works to bring a child into the world. With her into the birth space comes the preparatory work that she did, or did not, do, and the weight of expectations around what kind of a mother she will become, what kind of a birth she will have, and the web of relationships (with partners, family, friends) in which she is already positioned and known as a soon-to-be-mother. Even her own body is more than just one body: with biophysical actions and biochemical flows her body asserts its own agency, and there is a child-within who is also interacting with the process of labour and birth. The already networked woman at the centre of all this is the person who is expected to make choices about her care. As discussed in Chapter 1, the ability of women to make choices has for a long time been the focus of efforts to shift to more woman-centred models of care. But narratives of choice can place women in the difficult position of having to accept and take responsibility for all the consequences that flow from their decisions (Dombroski, McKinnon, & Healy, 2016). Just as important, however, are the choices around who and what to take as allies in the birth space, and how these allegiances can shape the experience of becoming a mother in unexpected ways—these relationships extend not just to human actors, but to the things we have around us. This chapter takes the example of the bed to explore the ways in which *objects* may also become actors within the birth space, with the relationships between people and things being forged through sometimes unexpected allegiances that produce (un)certain outcomes for women and babies.

The bed is caught up in a set of productive relationships, sharing a role in the birth space with the decision-making, thinking woman. Sitting in the centre of most birth wards, the bed calls a woman to lie down upon it, and this call may be welcomed, or it may be resisted, the bed may support a woman, or it may become an obstruction, even a prison. Thinking with Martin Heidegger's ruminations on the 'thingness of things', and Jane Bennett's ideas on 'thing-power', in this chapter I explore the idea that there is a 'bedness of the bed': the bed is its own entity (made by us, given purpose by its use, with its own presence) and at the same time, it moves us (or stills us) in particular ways—this inanimate thing in the room produces human action.

Thingness

The bed in the birthing space is much more than just an inanimate object, but there is limited language available for speaking about what this thing is and does. German philosopher, Martin Heidegger's famous 1967 book, *What Is a Thing?* provides one starting point. His essay begins with a whimsical nod to the long history of philosophers asking such frivolous questions as 'what is a thing?' Heidegger invokes Plato and the tale of a housemaid who laughed at the philosopher-astronomer Thales and admonished him for not attending to what was in front of his very nose and feet after he had fallen into a well, too preoccupied with studying the heavens. My sympathies lie with the housemaid, but Heidegger blithely dismisses her:

> ...the question "What is a thing?" must always be rated as one which causes housemaids to laugh. And genuine housemaids must have something to laugh about. ... [Philosophy] is that thinking with which one can start nothing and about which housemaids necessarily laugh. (Heidegger, 1967, p. 3)

Philosophy is not something for housemaids according to Heidegger. The stuff that is in front of your nose and your feet, the everyday concerns of keeping house, with aligned tasks of polishing shoes, washing laundry, and caring for children, are apparently not the stuff of high-minded contemplation. Luckily, we have Sara Ruddick to help us recognise the philosophical thinking at the core of these mundane practices, the theorizations that arise from reproductive labour and maternal work (Ruddick, 1989, see also discussion in Chapters 1 and 3). Misogyny aside, Heidegger's contemplations on what makes a thing a thing provide a helpful way to begin thinking about the stuff we are surrounded by, and which we must form relationships with, as we conduct our maternal work.

In asking what a thing is, Heidegger explores various possibilities: The things we encounter in daily life are simultaneously particular objects (my bed), and a stand in for all such objects (beds in general); they embody several truths at once (being simultaneously an object constructed of wood and fabric and nails and a carpenters measurements and calculation, and at the same time, the cosy nest of evening rest and chaotic family cuddles in the morning); they exist in relation to space and time; and, they carry their own properties (what the bed *is* is more than just what we make it, how we use it or perceive it—it is its own thing, it has its own nature). The idea that things have their own nature is easy to grasp for anyone who makes artefacts. The potter knows that to an extent the clay determines its own shape, the knitter knows that the wool has its own character, the carpenter must always work with the grain and the knots in the wood.

Once the thing is made, it still carries its own 'thingness,' that we must contend with in our encounters with it. Jane Bennett calls this 'thing-power':

> so-called inanimate things have a life... deep within is an inexplicable vitality or energy, a moment of independence from and resistance to us and other bodies: a kind of thing-power. (Bennett, 2010, p. 18)

We encounter thing-power in the contemporary world most often in the frequent reminders to be alert to the lifecycle of material goods. From the environmental impacts bound up in the manufacture of electronic devices, to the pollution and CO_2 produced through the use of the cars we own, to the harm caused by plastics as they enter the waste stream and become microplastics in the flesh of the fish we eat—the things we build and use and throw away have a life of their own that in turn impacts us and our planetary companions. Bennett explores this 'vital materiality' with which we share the world and provides a language with which to speak about the way that things 'impinge on us as much as we impinge on them' (2010, p. 115), even in the case of artefacts and commodities crafted by human hands.

In the transition to becoming a mother, thing-power is evident from the beginning. The stuff acquired for the work of baby care is often significant:

Prams and/or slings, nappies, wipes, muslins, pacifiers, onesies/vests. Bottles, breast pump(s), formula. Teething gel, nappy rash-cream, baby shoes-socks-mittens. Toys! Snacks, play mats. Tiny blankets, mattresses, fitted sheets, teddies, mobiles, night lights. For most non-poor denizens of advanced capitalist countries, the transition to parenthood involves becoming awash in a significantly new material landscape. (Boyer, 2018, p. 39)

Kate Boyer's research investigates the ways these things shape mothering. Her research explores the way prams shape how mother–baby dyads are able to move throughout the city. In effect, this means that the mobile mother becomes a mother-baby-pram assemblage that must relate with the environment in particular ways. Her interviews show that as a conjoined unit, mother-baby-pram discover a different urban geography: how you move through the streets, where you can go, and how you are received shift in different ways, and new mothers must negotiate their emerging maternal subjectivities though their 'entanglements with the more-than-human' (Boyer, 2018, pp. 50–51).

A mother's new entanglements with the more-than-human begins, of course, well before she hits the streets with her baby. In the interviews we conducted for this project an extensive catalogue of material objects were named: beds, chairs, birthing stools, bean bags, swiss balls, bars, tables, light switches, windows, doors, toilets, sinks, baths, showers, birth pools, mirrors, towels, curtains, floors, carpets, rugs, trolleys, gurneys, wheelchairs, resus units...and that's not even including any of the medical equipment.

But of all of these, the one thing present at almost every birth was the bed. Every single story we were told of a birth in hospital, and very many of the homebirths, included a bed. Those beds were seldom the inert bystanders one might expect.

What Is a (Birthing) Bed?

The bed might usually be associated with rest and repose, but it is also, of course, a thing made. It is steel and wood and fabric, composed into a frame and mattress, dressed with comforting blankets or draped in plastic that may be wiped down and sterilised. The beds in our birth stories sometimes have wheels and moving parts, sometimes they are wide, sometimes narrow. There is a creative intention behind their manufacture—who they are designed for and what they are designed to do, differs. The mind that designed them, the hands and machinery that built them, have left an imprint. The bed is also a product of labour, something made, if not by artisanal labour then by workers in a factory who are selling their labour in exchange for a wage. In the birthing suite, the bed is caught up in a different set of productive relationships. The means through which it was crafted are no longer visible but the 'thing-power' of a bed carries traces of its manufacture and the intention with which it was crafted.

For centuries the bed has been an object of stature and status. For those with the means to pay, enormous time, effort and expense went into making a bed. From the British Isles to Beijing, for more privileged members of society, the bed was a massive object, made from precious woods or metals, decorated with shell inlays, with silver and gold, made comfortable by mattresses of feathers, wool and hair, dressed with linen and silk (Wright, 1962). In the seventeenth century the marital bed was often commissioned for the newlywed couple, and built in situ of heavy timber. One of the few items Shakespeare's wife, Anne Hathaway, was bequeathed in the will was the wedding bed. This was not the snub it is sometimes thought to be: unlike today, the marital bed was a significant asset in the household, with considerable status and symbolic value, 'In any house, the bed was the most costly item of furniture and sometimes so massive and heavy that it could hardly be regarded as moveable property… a big bed could be worth as much as a small house' (Greer, 2011). The marital bed was a prestige investment for newlyweds, and a major asset of the household.

Newlyweds may have conceived in the bed, but it was seldom a place where women gave birth. The very earliest records of childbirth show women upright, often squatting or kneeling. One of the oldest depictions dates back to 69-30 BC: it is a bas-relief on the wall of the Temple of Esneh in Egypt, and depicts a kneeling Cleopatra, giving birth with five female attendants (Dundes, 1987). Until the fifteenth and sixteenth centuries, a much more common piece of furniture used in childbirth was the birthing chair, various versions of which have been used around the world, with the oldest record dating back to Babylonian times in 2000 BC. Amanda Carson Banks reveals how, throughout history, the birthing chair reflects changing ideology and practice, as childbirth transformed from a process in which women sought the support of other women, to a dangerous 'disease state' and 'the province of medical specialists' (1999, pp. xxi–xxii). In the 1600s Francois Muriceáu advocated the benefits of the reclining position for childbirth. According to Anthony Reid and Nancy Harris, Muriceáu 'represented the new wave of barber surgeons who had become part of obstetrics in their role as assistants at difficult deliveries, and who valued the easier access to the perineum provided by the horizontal position' (1988, p. 1994).

Legend has it that it was King Louis XIV of France who popularised the use of the bed in childbirth, however. Breaking conventions of the day that kept fathers out of the birthing room, the king was curious to observe his mistress, Louise de la Valliére, giving birth to their child. Louis placed himself behind a curtain, but disappointed that he could not see very much, insisted that la Valliere be lain on the bed, exposed, so that he could see the baby emerge. According to Janet Leiberman, this example sparked the French nobility to follow suit, popularising the idea that women should lie reclining on their backs to give birth and bringing birth 'out into the open, sans petticoats'. Leiberman claims that, as a result, the science of midwifery and obstetrics could at last be developed' (Lieberman, 1976, p. 44).

One of the key instruments in the advancement of this 'science' was the invention of forceps, first used by the Chamberlen brothers in the 1600s. The brothers kept their invention a secret and went to extraordinary lengths to keep it so, blindfolding the labouring mother and locking family members and attendants out of the room while it was put to use (Dunn, 1999; Sheikh, Ganesaratnam, & Jan, 2013). As anaesthesia and the use of forceps became increasingly common through the eighteenth and nineteenth centuries, male surgeons increasingly practised 'man-midwifery' (Sheikh et al., 2013), and women were more commonly encouraged to lie down during childbirth. The bed in the birth space thus became a tool of exposure and an ally in the emergence of the technologies of obstetric intervention.

As obstetrics advanced, so the bed transformed in accordance with shifting conventions. By the mid–late 1800s the practice of lying a woman down flat on her back (rather than propped up in a reclining position) and placing her feet in stirrups—the 'lithotomy' position—was beginning to be adopted much more widely, particularly in the United States (Dundes, 1987). What drove the change was the convenience of the attending physician. Doctor William Dewees in 1828 stated, for example, that 'the woman should be placed so as to give the least possible hinderance to the operations of the accoucheur—this is agreed upon by all' (cited by Dundes, 1987, p. 639). The invention of an adjustable hospital bed soon followed. By 1938 Mr Stanton Marchbanks was issued a patent for a bed that could be adjusted, with the end removed to allow access to the lower body, and footbeds attached, or posts mounted 'in order that the legs may be strapped thereto during the operation, examination or treatment of portions of the body in the region of the pelvis' (United States Patent Office, 1942). The hospital birthing bed had emerged as a thing that already had opinions about how a woman should give birth and what placement of her body would allow the easiest access.

The 'Thing-Power' of the Bed

Today, the fact that it is easier to see what is happening if a woman is exposed and lying on her back, is why many doctors still think the prone position (lithotomy) works best for childbirth. Michael, speaking on the verge of his retirement as a GP-Obstetrician in New Zealand, was one of those who much preferred women to give birth on the bed:

> *Some women want to deliver on the floor. I hate the floor, because getting down on your knees is difficult. You don't have a good view, and I just - I can't do it. Just getting down there is awful. It doesn't work for me. … Sometimes they'll do it standing up and you've got to try and catch it, so that the baby doesn't get a head injury afterwards, worries me too… If they're on the floor when I get there, with the midwives on their knees down there, I say fine…I leave them to it. But when things are going wrong, I say on the bed please.*

The doctor, whose job it is to step in when things are going wrong, prefers the clear view to a woman's vulva that is facilitated by the birthing bed. In this, the bed does work for the doctor. As Michael goes on to note:

The so-called stranded beetle position [is] in fact a good position, because (a) you can get your knees up almost to your ears, (b) you've got really good vision and you can see the perineum. Because what you're trying to do is guard the perineum, so it doesn't tear.... You've got really good position to keep the head not coming down too fast. You don't want it coming out like a cannonball, because that's when you tear. So, you're trying to keep things back, and slow the delivery to allow it to stretch. So, I like people lying on their backs.

Because it is a bed—a thing made to lie upon—and because women often expect to give birth lying down, the very presence of the bed in the room calls a woman to lie down. In doing so it produces a patient out of a birthing woman. It is an object built for a prone body, and it is not surprising then that so many women feel obliged to lie down. His assertion that the prone position avoids tears could be disputed (Dahlen et al., 2007), but to allow a clear view and accessibility the prone position is ideal for a doctor like Michael.

For the woman, however, lying down is often not ideal. Women once routinely gave birth strapped into stirrups, often their hands were also strapped down also and while in this vulnerable position they were made to have their pubic hair shaved and their bowels evacuated by enema. In the case of 'twilight sleep' obstetric intervention also involved administering doses of morphine and scopolamine (hyoscine) in combination so as to render a labouring mother unconscious while forceps were used to deliver the baby. Joseph De Lee advised in 1920 that obstetricians should apply this approach to eliminate the pain of first stage labour and eliminate the second stage of labour altogether by surgical forceps delivery (De Lee, 1920). The practice of imposing manual delivery, rather than allowing a woman to deliver her own baby was based on a misguided sense that women were suffering needlessly. According to Simons, DeLee 'compared labour to being impaled with a pitchfork for the woman, and for the infant, to having its head caught in a door (De Lee, 1920, pp. 39–40). ... Ideally, he advised, women should be rendered unconscious so they could not interfere with doctors' manual extraction of babies' (Simonds, 2002, p. 561).

This treatment of women has since been characterised as 'birth rape' (Mardorossian, 2014; Richland, 2008; Shabot, 2016), although it is argued elsewhere that 'consumer demand' drove the use of twilight sleep (Leavitt, 1980; Moscucci, 2003). Twilight sleep is a thing of the past, but the stirrups remain. This prone position allows carers easy access to a woman's vagina, and this is important when obstetric interventions such as an episiotomy, ventouse or forceps delivery need to be used.

The prone position, however, is not conducive to the descent of the child or to the opening of a pelvis which needs to flex in order to allow a baby's head to pass through. The World Health Organization recommends against lithotomy for second-stage labour. Several studies have shown that upright or side-lying positions help the pelvis to open and are 'associated with a shorter duration of second-stage labour, fewer forceps or vacuum births, fewer episiotomies, fewer abnormal foetal heart rate patterns, and less chance of having severe pain during pushing' (Lothian, 2009, p. 51, see also Gupta, Hofmeyr, & Smyth, 2004). It is now widely accepted that upright positions are best because they enable more efficient contractions; shorter labour; better oxygenation of the baby in the mother's uterus, as the blood supply is not compressed by the pregnant uterus; increased pelvic diameter, especially in positions such as squatting; less maternal pain; greater satisfaction; fewer forceps, vacuum births, and episiotomies (Dahlen, 2013). And, of course, these positions make better use of gravity to help the baby descend. While the bed might call a woman to lie down, the go-go-gadget bed of the delivery ward is not proving itself an ally to the natural processes of labour and vaginal birth. Timing is everything—unless obstetric intervention becomes necessary, the bed is likely to work *against* a woman's body instead of working with it.

The thing-power of the bed is thus more allied with the obstetrical actors in the room (the forceps, the episiotomy scissors, and the hands of those that wield them). Michael notes that a good delivery bed has to be '*movable into various shapes and positions... You need to be able to get rid of the bottom of the bed, and you need to have various places to put legs. Because what you've got to do is be able to get at the bits and pieces that are important to get at*'. With the access afforded by the bed, other objects also become relevant: '*You need to have a really good light*'. And close to hand the instruments that might be needed: '*your suturing material, your local anaesthetic - all that sort of thing*'. The birthing bed can be understood as an agent in a gathering network of allied objects, which in turn support a set of practices that include the obstetric interventions of medical staff and the lying down of a woman.

ALLIES AND ANTAGONISMS

At the same time as the birthing bed gathers allies, it also prompts adversarial gatherings and engagements. For many women, lying down does not feel like a good way to give birth and in these circumstances the bed becomes something to be negotiated with, the work it does contested. Susan Ross is a prominent childbirth educator and doula trainer in New South Wales, Australia. Over many years of supporting women through their births, both at home and in hospital, she spoke at length about the way that the bed shapes a birth experience:

> *Well, I think one of the big things in the space is I would like to remove is the bed. The bed's a huge obstacle in a delivery suite. A couple of years ago I was at a birth in a private hospitall – one of those women who really, probably, should have had her baby at home. She realised that at about 37 weeks of pregnancy – impossible to change, unfortunately.*
>
> *So we went with this and ... she said 'oh, that bed. They just expect you to get on it', which they did do in this private hospital. So I actually wheeled the bed out in the corridor... She had a beautiful rug that she'd brought in herself. We had lots of pillows and cushions and stuff. There was no room to move the bed back in.*

In this case Susan and the mother she was caring for shunted aside the bed and its allies by filling the space with an alternative coalition of objects: rug, pillows, cushions, stuff. This gentle form of resistance to the thing-power of the bed made possible a different set of practices in the room, crucially shaping the position in which the mother could deliver her child.

In other circumstances, however, the thing-power of the bed was applied too forcefully to be resisted. Miranda gave birth to her first baby in the United Kingdom. After an uncomplicated pregnancy, she was hopeful of a straightforward, natural labour. Having read about what to expect, she was aware that being mobile during her labour was likely to help the pain and ease the progression of labour. But when she arrived at hospital, she discovered that the bed in the room did not just call to her, it became her prison:

> *I went into [laughs] the birthing room and literally was told to be on the bed the whole time... There was space there to walk around and move, but I was literally told to get back on the bed when I got off the bed... The nurses from the station would come to the window and look in, and if I was on the bed they would just*

leave me. When I got off the bed to do yoga in a rather oversized Miffy shirt with no underpants on, someone did come in and tell me to get back on the bed [laughs]. So... it was quite dogmatic. I literally felt like I was in some sort of prison.

The bed is not always a prison however. A bed can also be a thing that provides support for the kneeling, leaning, resting through the labour—whether in a hospital or at home. Mary was brought up in the country, and her first introduction to childbirth was at the age of 11 when she saw her younger brother born at home. Asked how this may have shaped her expectations around childbirth Mary reflected that:

It made me a lot more relaxed about giving birth, it wasn't such a freaky thing. I think with Mum, she had six of us, my older sister and my youngest brother were both born at home accidentally. I always just thought that since Mum had her first baby, out on the [country] ... well it just made me think that it's a real natural thing and our bodies are made to do it and even if we don't know what we're doing it's going to happen in the end. All natural.

When Mary had her own children, she chose to have a homebirth under the New Zealand public health care system. Her partner was not so happy with the decision, and her midwife was not experienced in homebirth, but since she lived only one block away from the hospital, both were convinced to support her. The bed played a pivotal role. Her first baby was born in the bedroom, 'it was quite small bed and we just pushed the bed up against the wall and made some room. She was just born beside the bed'. Squashed into the tiny bedroom with her were her partner, her midwife, and her mother. The second time around things were similarly intimate. This time she was joined in the bedroom by her partner, her mother, her midwife, her eldest child, and her 12-year-old niece stationed at the doorway. As a Maori woman, it was important to her to have her family gathered around. Her baby was born on the bed:

We tried on my knees and moving around, all sorts of places...it was much harder. So Hana was seven pound, four, and Ari was nine pound eight. So it was a lot harder, and I was just exhausted, so I couldn't hold myself up on my knees. So that's why we ended up on the bed.

The crowded room was part of what made the experience special for her. It provided comfort and reassurance: '*It was really nice to have other people there, especially with having Hana, like not having to worry about her*'.

For Mary, her bed did the work of providing rest and support during a difficult and tiring birth. And with her family gathered around as she gave birth on it, the bed also helped to form the space in which to become a family: with siblings and cousins and grandparents also playing an active role to provide support and reassurance. These forms of support were given alongside the interventions that then became necessary. Mary reflected that in this second birth the midwife played a much more active role '*because Ari got a bit stuck coming out so having that medical knowledge and her telling me to stop pushing and that sort of thing, that was [important]*'. In this case, a medical intervention was still possible in a space in which the bed was allied, not with a doctor and his obstetric technologies, but with a mother and her carers, working together to achieve a 'natural' birth. For Mary, getting on the bed did not have to mean being strapped into a lithotomy position, disciplined into immobility, or imprisoned.

Conclusion

The bed's presence in the birth space *does* something, it shapes that space in particular ways which in turn shape a woman's experience of birth. It gifts sturdy sides as support, it calls the woman in labour to lie upon it; it holds her in comfort; it betrays her, becoming a frame that displays her for a doctor's benefit. The bed is a thing made by human hands, but it also has a life and agency of its own, which shapes the birth space in particular ways.

To be attentive to the agency of the bed itself and the way it is caught up in complex relationships, highlights the ways that the space of birth, and the *things* in that space, may have tangible effects on the experience of birth. The implications of what things are present are not always immediately obvious: what does it mean to get on the bed, what implications for the unfolding birth does this simple action carry, how is power over oneself and one's child shifted by the interventions that the bed itself makes possible? These are the opaque consequences that flow from allegiances formed or denied with objects in the birth space. Such allegiances can displace the power and agency of the individual woman who is becoming a mother. But it may also mean that objects, the stuff in the birthing space, can be enrolled into strategic coalitions—ones that may enable greater control of a woman over her body. The bed may be moved into the hallway or a woman may allow herself to be strapped to it—each signalling a very different engagement with the agency of the bed and a different set of associated power relations between a mother and her carers. The childbirth assemblage is not, then, a flat expanse of connected actors. The set of connections that form around any given birth take shape through negotiations of power, positioning a mother and baby in different ways in relation to those that are caring for them. A childbirth assemblage comes into being inflected with the competing (or allied) expectations and values of a mother and those animate and inanimate actors present to support her through the birth.

REFERENCES

Bennett, J. (2010). *Vibrant matter: A political ecology of things*. Durham and London: Duke University Press.

Boyer, K. (2018). *Spaces and politics of motherhood*. London: Rowman & Littlefield.

Dahlen, H. (2013, May 7). Stand and deliver—Upright births best for mum and bub. *The Conversation*, p. 4.

Dahlen, H., Homer, C. S. E., Cooke, M., Upton, A. M., Nunn, R., & Brodrick, B. (2007). Perineal outcomes and maternal comfort related to the application of perineal warm packs in the second stage of labor: A randomized controlled trial. *Birth, 34*(4), 282–290. https://doi.org/10.1111/j.1523-536X.2007.00186.x.

De Lee, J. B. (1920). *The principles and practice of obstetrics*. Philadelphia: WB Saunders Company.

Dombroski, K., McKinnon, K., & Healy, S. (2016). Beyond the birth wars: Diverse assemblages of care. *New Zealand Geographer, 72*, 230–239. https://doi.org/10.1111/nzg.12142.

Dundes, L. (1987). The evolution of maternal birthing position. *American Journal of Public Health, 77*(5), 6.

Dunn, P. M. (1999). The Chamberlen family (1560–1728) and obstetric forceps. *Archives of Disease in Childhood—Fetal and Neonatal Edition, 81*(3), F232–F234. https://doi.org/10.1136/fn.81.3.F232.

Greer, G. (2011). *Shakespeare's wife*. ebook: A&C Black.

Gupta, J. K., Hofmeyr, G. J., & Smyth, R. (2004). Position in the second stage of labour for women without epidural anaesthesia. *Cochrane Database of Systematic Reviews*, Issue 1. Art. No. CD002006. https://doi.org/10.1002/14651858.CD002006.pub2.

Heidegger, M. (1967). *What is a thing?* Chicago: Henry Regnery Company.

Leavitt, J. W. (1980). Birthing and anesthesia: The debate over twilight sleep. *Signs: Journal of Women in Culture and Society, 6*(1), 147–164.

Lieberman, J. J. (1976). Childbirth practices: From darkness into light. *Journal of Obstetric, Gynecologic, and Neonatal Nursing, 5*(3), 41–45. https://doi.org/10.1111/j.1552-6909.1976.tb02306.x.

Lothian, J. A. (2009). Safe, healthy birth: What every pregnant woman needs to know. *The Journal of Perinatal Education, 18*(3), 48–54. http://dx.doi.org.ez.library.latrobe.edu.au/10.1624/105812409X461225.

Mardorossian, C. M. (2014). *Framing the Rape Victim: Gender and Agency Reconsidered*. New Brunswick, NJ and London: Rutgers University Press.

Moscucci, O. (2003). Holistic obstetrics: The origins of "natural childbirth" in Britain. *Postgraduate Medical Journal, 79*(929), 168–173. https://doi.org/10.1136/pmj.79.929.168.

Reid, A. J., & Harris, N. L. (1988). Alternative birth positions. *Canadian Family Physician, 34,* 1993–1998.

Richland, S. (2008). Birth rape: Another midwife's story. *Midwifery Today*, Spring, 42–43.

Ruddick, S. (1989). *Maternal thinking: Towards a politics of peace*. New York: Ballantine Books.

Shabot, S. C. (2016). Making loud bodies "feminine": A feminist-phenomenological analysis of obstetric violence. *Human Studies, 39*(2), 231–247. https://doi.org/10.1007/s10746-015-9369-x.

Sheikh, S., Ganesaratnam, I., & Jan, H. (2013). The birth of forceps. *JRSM Short Reports, 4*(7), 1–4. https://doi.org/10.1177/2042533313478412.

Simonds, W. (2002). Watching the clock: Keeping time during pregnancy, birth, and postpartum experiences. *Social Science & Medicine, 55*(4), 559–570. https://doi.org/10.1016/S0277-9536(01)00196-4.

United States Patent Office. (1942). 'Hospital Bed', Patent 2,275,973. Cattanooga, Tenn: Marchbanks.

Wright, L. (1962). *Warm and snug: The history of the bed*. London: Routledge & Kegan Paul.

CHAPTER 5

Doctoring with Bureaucracy

Abstract This chapter draws on the reflections of midwives and obstetricians speaking about their negotiations between rigid policy and the more fluid and unpredictable circumstances of giving birth. The policies themselves, and the legal advisors and actuaries who inform policy, the bureaucrats who formalise them, and the managers who police them, are all invisible but powerful presences in the birth space. Their presence can be a challenge for obstetricians, midwives, and mothers who are unwilling to blindly follow policy in place of well-informed, empathetic, and responsive practices of care. The negotiations that must take place across a birth assemblage must therefore include the invisible but present influence of key institutions, represented in the birth space by the blank forms that must be filled in, recording progress, interventions and clinical outcomes.

Keywords Bureaucracy · Policy · Regulation · Litigation · Loving care · Gaming the system

My first baby was meant to have been born at home. The signs looked good but after more than 2 and a half hours of pushing my midwives wanted me to move to hospital. 'We need to monitor the baby. The rules say we're only supposed to let you push for 2 hours at home. We're sorry'. I was beyond knowing what to do other than just follow their advice. Well into 'labour land' I was not capable of thinking or articulating very much at all. On the way to the car the contractions started coming fast and strong, but on we pressed through an agonising drive to the hospital, and a wheelchair ride through the waiting room with happy families celebrating new arrivals – me kneeling on the wheelchair, ruddy faced and dishevelled, fluid dripping through my clothes, utterly undignified. In hospital I was moved onto the bed in the centre of the room, my feet lifted into the stirrups. By now my body had taken over pushing hard without any conscious effort from me. Slowly slowly, millimetre by millimetre the baby moved downwards. Not fast enough for the obstetrician. My mother, watching, saw my three midwives form a scrum around the bed; finding reasons to obstruct the doctors view and delay her interference. But finally, they had to stand aside, and all I remember is the doctor leaning in between my splayed legs with a needle in one hand and a scalpel in the other saying, "I'm just going to give you a little cut." At that very moment a contraction took me, and my daughter crowned. Two more pushes and she was out, sounding extremely cross. She nestled onto my chest and latched on for her first hearty drink (she still loves her food). And I didn't tear at all. Her timing saved me from an unnecessary, unwanted, and un-consented to episiotomy.

Midwives attending a homebirth in New Zealand are governed, as are all midwives, by a carefully laid out set of recommended policies and guidelines. When my second stage had extended well past the time limits of the guidelines, the presence of their governing force became tangible in the room. I had to go to hospital. And in hospital, the birth plan I had worked out with my midwives, that stated explicitly that I would rather tear than receive an episiotomy, was no longer relevant—it was as if it no longer existed.

The presence of the recommended policies and guidelines in the birth space are invisible to most of those present, but midwives and obstetricians carry the knowledge of them everywhere they go. One midwife described this to me as a dark and ominous cloud that follows you around. It is dark and ominous because while the regulations are based on averages, an individual woman's experience may be at the far end of the spectrum of what is normal or safe. It is seldom that any individual experience adheres to a population average—regardless of what is being measured. But in maternity care, when a woman does not conform to the average, the regulations insist that carers should take action. Midwives must then respond, both to the woman who they are caring for, and to the 'norms' established by regulations.

This delicate balancing act is akin to what Annemarie Mol describes in her work with diabetes patients and the doctors and nurses who care for them (2008). Mol describes the way that the 'logic of choice' that dominates health care would have us believe that choices about care are made rationally, based on facts and evidence. But the actual practice of health care that Mol witnesses is something very different. Decisions about monitoring blood sugar levels, managing diet and exercise, undergoing various treatments, are all made around much more than just 'facts'. Care regimes must be determined iteratively, around an individual's life circumstances, preference, and experience, and a doctor's ability to empathise, encourage, and inform. 'Facts' about how diabetes should be managed, and evidence about what practices lead to better outcomes, are based again on averages. But an individual's care regimes must be shaped around that individual, their life and livelihood. As Mol points out:

> In a logic of choice all fluidity is located in the moment choices are being made. At that moment the facts are given, and so too are the possible courses of action. But the way the various values involved will add together has yet to crystallise. What to do? This or that, A or B? (Mol, 2008, p. 58)

The shaping of care around a particular person's life requires something different. Something that Mol argues fits better with a 'logic of care' as opposed to a 'logic of choice'. What is different is that 'care' recognises the relationality at the heart of doctors and patients figuring out what is going to succeed and what is not:

> Somehow technology, daily habits and people's skills and propensities have all to be mutually adjusted. This is crucial in the logic of care. It is important to attune everything to everything else. Nothing is taken to be entirely fixed or entirely fluid. Technologies, habits, hopes, everything in a patient's life may have to be adjusted. (Mol, 2008, p. 61)

The process of adjusting, of responding to what works and what does not, is a process of experimentation: 'Care is not a matter of implementing knowledge and technology, but of experimenting with them' (Mol, 2008, p. 64). The work involved here is the work of *doctoring*.

Mol's description of doctoring might well be applied to what my midwives were practising as my labours stalled. They were adjusting and experimenting, trying again, tinkering. Doctoring is about 'being knowledgeable, accurate and skilful' but it also involves being 'attentive, inventive, persistent and forgiving' (Mol 2008, p. 64). And it is something that is done in teams—it is not just a doctor who doctors. That process of trying, testing, adjusting, is necessarily a shared project in which doctors, nurses, technologies, patients all contribute. It is, according to Mol, a shared endeavour of balancing evidence and facts with values and lived experience.

In this chapter, I explore Mol's concept of 'doctoring' to think about the practice of 'midwifing'. There is much to balance in the process of caring for a woman in childbirth: a woman's values, her baby's health, family expectations, the knowledge and experience of past births, a set of normative 'facts' and associated guidelines, the regulatory gaze of the nurses board or hospital management, the information emanating from monitoring devices, and so on. For many of the midwives and obstetricians we interviewed, however, a preoccupying issue was how to negotiate the mismatch between rigid policy and the more fluid and unpredictable circumstances of giving birth. This chapter explores this concern, and the way that 'midwifing' is practised alongside the invisible but inescapable inflexibility of rules and regulations.

Bureaucracy

Policies, procedures, regulations, guidelines, the record-keeping that accompanies them, the monitoring and review systems that enforce them, the hierarchies of accountability and decision-making that enact them, come together as one many-headed creature in our contemporary world. That creature is called bureaucracy. Professor of theoretical medicine at the University of Buckingham, Bruce Charlton, likens bureaucracy to the Borg in Star Trek, 'it feeds upon and assimilates opposition' with all attempts to 'cut red tape' or 'create efficiencies' in management resulting in 'more and bigger bureaucracies' and ever-decreasing degrees of rationality and functionality, in contrast to the bureaucracies that existed when Weber did his famous analysis of them (Charlton, 2010, pp. 962–963). As Kathleen Eastman and Martha Loustaunau have pointed out, any birth that takes place in a hospital is taking place in a medical bureaucracy, with the hierarchy of authority, the system of rules, and impersonality that this entails (Eastman & Loustaunau, 1988).

While enacted, shaped, and performed in a myriad of different ways in different locations, there is something cohesive about the bureaucracies of maternity care. The way bureaucratic process enters the birth space, how professionals feel both obliged to it and sometimes fearful of it, and the ways mothers are expected to acquiesce to it, are remarkably similar across the very different maternity care settings of Australia and New Zealand (and the literature also suggests similar relationships in the United States, Britain, and probably elsewhere). As Eastman and Loustaunau argue, bureaucratic hierarchies privilege policies and procedures convenient to them rather than to the patients they serve, while patients are expected to take a passive role (1988). Similarly, Hoag described bureaucracies as 'confounding' entities, 'because their laws, rules, and regulations all fundamentally prescribe or proscribe behaviour of an ideal, universal, and abstract sort' (2011, p. 82). Bureaucracies categorise complex things so they fit within neat boundaries, establish procedures that must always be followed, and strict hierarchies of decision-making to ensure uniformity. As Hoag points out, the set of regulations describe an ideal that is never entirely present in reality. The work to attain the ideal is a practice of 'masking the exercise of power in the guise of an always emergent—but never attained—perfect order'. Citing Donna Haraway's term, he says, 'this production of universality is the "god trick" of bureaucracies, the illusion of even, unmediated, and rational vision' (Hoag, 2011, p. 82); the 'god trick' creates an illusion of objectivity and rationality. In the case of maternity bureaucracies this means outlining the progressive steps and timing through which labour is 'meant' to occur, and prescribing interventions. The problem with this is that it leaves little room for 'midwifing', for adjusting and responding, for allowing the fluid and unpredictable unfolding of an individual woman's labours.

FEAR AND CONTROL IN MATERNAL BUREAUCRACIES

James, the chief obstetrician of a maternity unit at a hospital in an affluent neighbourhood of Sydney, spoke at length about the challenges of working to the protocols rather than working to the woman:

> *I think that's the power of the climate of apprehension and fear … There's a very strong emphasis on having protocols around… and make sure this is attended to and that attended to and then it becomes so constrained that after a while people – we lose sight of what might be individually necessary for some women. Or the ability to individualise things in a responsible way gets squashed or gets viewed as a bit left wing and airy fairy.*

The balancing act between meeting a woman's needs and practising to the protocols is at one level the balancing act between giving space and time for labour to unfold and ensuring that it does not edge over into a space of potential danger (discussed more in Chapter 7). But the key point James was making was that he saw his own staff struggle with the apprehension and fear that an expectation of adhering to protocols can create. This fear leads professionals to intervene before they should, take action when the woman herself does not need it, or lean in to 'give a little cut' when it is not called for: Better to do something than be seen to have done nothing. When something does go wrong and you are called to account, the best a doctor can do is to show that she did her utmost to deliver the baby safely. The utmost is almost always a caesarean delivery.

It is not only clinical staff who must adhere to the protocols, but also women. In our interviews we heard many stories of policies, regulation, and guidelines, ostensibly in place to protect women and ensure safe care practice, being used instead to police women (as well as their carers). Laura is a Sydney mother who had given birth twice in hospital under the care of the same private obstetrician, with her last baby born at home. For both hospital births she began her antenatal care very clear that she wanted to try for a natural birth, but ended up with caesarean deliveries; one was scheduled, the other followed a labour that 'failed to progress'. In both instances her immediate feeling was one of both disappointment and frustration, yet reconciliation to an experience that was retold to friends and family as positive. After her first birth she recalls:

> So, for me to have just gone in and come home with a baby, and I had a really good recovery physically – to me it just seemed like it was a positive experience. So that was just what I would tell people – it was a positive experience, it was positive experience, and we're healthy and that's all that matters.

But in hindsight, her perspective shifted considerably. Through both stories what she recalled most powerfully were the feelings of disempowerment:

> It's like you just don't feel like you're a person with any decision-making power. You're just this object, they just make the decisions for you and tell you how it's going to be.

This feeling emerged not only from a process that ended with an unwanted caesarean, but the way she and her body were treated along the way. Alongside recalling the kindness and humanity of the anaesthetist, who was a '*beautiful man*' and '*the kind of doctor that makes you feel like a person*', Laura's overwhelming memory was of feeling dehumanised:

> *When I was still in theatre, bright lights everywhere and unfamiliar faces and there's – I could feel pain and I could feel like I was kind of being pushed around a bit. And I'm – because the sheet's still up – I'm like, what is going on? This woman leans over and she's scrubbing my stomach like this and she's says to me, it's okay, I just clean, I just clean. I'm there going, well that kind of hurts, so that's not okay. Yes, I may have had an epidural but I'm still a person and you don't scrub me like a piece of stone. But it just, it wasn't nice.*

After this experience Laura was even more adamant to have a natural birth the second time around. The signs were good. During a routine check with her obstetrician she was beginning to dilate, and the baby was in position, but at 38 weeks already the obstetrician was recommending induction. Before that could happen, her waters broke, and when the midwives at the hospital found out who her doctor was, they told her she had to come in and be admitted. Knowing this could lead again to another caesarean, she resisted, and was supported in her resistance by the midwives. Like the scrum that formed to protect me from an unnecessary episiotomy, the midwives at her hospital found ways to give her more space to birth:

> *...you could tell that the midwives were coming from the same angle I was – that things happen better on their own. But they couldn't advise me, because my doctor wanted me admitted. So they were saying to me, she wants us to find you a room, maybe you could disappear for a couple of hours because we're having a problem finding a room. Maybe you could just, you know, hop in your car and go somewhere and – but don't go too far, not too far, because if we need you to be here, we're going to let you know. I said, okay. So we didn't go too far, because we didn't want to break the rules.*

As she had feared, she ended up with a second caesarean. Along the way, the story she told was of a litany of small moments of bullying and disrespect: being forced to take medicine she didn't want because '*no, no, all of [Karen's] patients take them, take these tablets. ...The doctor's asked you to take them, you take them*'; to being monitored because it was 'hospital policy':

You can't get in the bath because you need to be monitored. I'm sorry, I know you don't want to be monitored, but that's the hospital policy.

Eventually, with no conversation about consent or explanation of why or how it had become vital, she found herself wheeled into the operating theatre again.

She checked and she said, You're three centimetres and this is a problem. I'll need to ring your doctor… Then I turned into a pleading woman: But I'll rest, I'll do whatever you want. Just don't – don't do this. She's like, No, I just need to ring her and let her know… She walks [back] in and says she'll be here shortly to do a C-section.

Following the birth of her second child, the baby was taken to the neonatal unit. From the moment of birth Laura was under the impression that she had come very close to harming her baby because of her desire to birth naturally. When she opened Laura up, the obstetrician said, 'Oh my God!':

I opened my eyes and was like, what? The cord was around Harry's neck. When she held him up and showed him to me, he was very purple. James wasn't like that when he was born, so I instantly panicked. They were holding him there, showing him to me. I said take him, take him away, because if something's wrong – all I could think was, if I have selfishly pushed for a natural birth and it has been to the detriment of my son, I will never forgive myself, and because he just, he looked a bit purple. I said take him away, like, help him, help him please. Don't just stand there showing him to me. So the midwife took him, cleaned him up, wrapped him up, gave him a bit of oxygen and then again, I said to Matt, go be with him, because I was just in sheer panic at this point thinking something's going to be wrong and it's all my fault, it's all my fault.

Later Laura learned that it is very normal to have the cord wrapped around the neck, but at the time she did not know that, so when they only let her see her baby for a brief time, she did not object. Having birthed on Saturday, finally on Monday she was allowed to try breastfeeding, after her baby had already been fed formula through a nasal tube rather than being allowed to access his mother's milk:

I went in and they said it's rest time, you can't have anybody in here with you and my friend was visiting. So I said, can I take him to my room to feed and they said, yes, and I never took him back. I stole my baby. But I knew the paediatrician who was looking after him… the nurses from special care went and got him when I refused to take Harry back to special care.

He came in to see me and I said, this baby needs to be with his mother. I said he needs to be breastfed, he needs to be held, he doesn't need to be sat in a bassinet in a special care nursery by himself. Doctor [X] was like, You're right. You're exactly right. It was funny, because the special care midwife's standing there going, but, but. And he was like, he's doing fine, he's feeding fine, he can stay with her. He signed something to say that he was discharging the baby to me. I thought, jeez, I should have tried that on Saturday.

The ordered structure of care, with regulated times for rest, protocols for where a baby should be and when, and a responsiveness not to the mother and child themselves but to the commands of someone further up the hierarchy—these are all the quiet entry points of maternal bureaucracy. Only by a successful negotiation with someone high enough up the chain of accountability could the mother and baby be allowed to stay together.

Laura's third child was born at home under the care of an independent midwife, and her experience of that birth was very different (a story I tell in Chapter 7). The story of her first two births, however, is a story about the way that a birth bureaucracy, unseen and unacknowledged, was playing a part in the inexorable steps taken towards an unwanted caesarean: First the hierarchies at play that make the doctor's word like the word of god, and second the invocation of 'policy' to police a woman into accepting something that she probably could have safely refused. Her reflection on what was different about birthing at home is insightful:

The whole time I was just focused on me, which was the difference. When I was in labour with Harry, I was too busy being afraid, looking around thinking, Who's going to come and get me? This time I was just… in my bedroom, I was just focusing on getting through each 60 seconds and then resting again.

This is the fear that policy and protocol produce, not just for the midwives who cannot care as they feel they should, or for the doctor, who might suggest inductions and recommend caesarean when they aren't yet clinically indicated, but also the fear it promotes in a mother who has been told, if she does not reach a set target by a set time, she will be cut open.

Litigation and the 'Cerebral'

The other side of fear is a concern to protect. This applies to protecting both the mother and the professional. The presence of the bureaucracy compels professionals to behave in certain ways and follow decisions that might adhere to policy but do not always adhere well with best practice. A senior midwife and midwife educator said to me recently that, 'it's as if sometimes the hierarchy is more important than life and death'. Sally, one of the few independent midwives working the Sydney basin, reflected on the nature of the hospital:

> ... at home it's the woman's house and I'm the guest, but you're going to hospital and immediately you're the guest there. It's the hospital's domain. They ... try to be welcoming but it's only to a point. It's only as long as you're going to play by their rules.
>
> If you have decided not to make certain compromises and have decided to say no, they get really upset by that. It's like, Why won't you? This is the rule. You should be doing this. Then the – it's the staff that get angry. So then it all spirals down from there, and that takes away from the woman's experience.

'Playing by the rules' can leave a woman feeling, as Laura did, disempowered and regretful. And it does not meet the needs of a woman in the throes of labour. James, the obstetrician we met earlier, reflected at length about the contrasts between the way the institutions of care function, and the actual needs of women who are in labour. James spoke about his observations of the way that a labouring woman 'has to focus on herself',

> She's got this task that's so strong that that almost... gives her an exclusion zone around her which says look you've got to be quiet here and I don't necessarily want to be touched ...and so you've just got to work with it [especially with women who are] in a particular zone that's not quite the sort of conscious way we're – so you and I are talking now, it's something different.

In contrast to the 'zone' around a woman, and the way that labour calls her to space of maternal consciousness, that is not 'cerebral', the clinical space:

> centres around the concept of a patient, very much a conscious patient, who is making decisions and therefore ... the role of the birthing unit is to make everything safe in a very conscious way. It's evidence-based. It's very cerebral

and it's so cerebral that when consideration about what we're talking about – women being zoned [out] – that almost gets dismissed as, well it is dismissed as oh it's a bit airy fairy and really you need to be on top of (x), (y) and (z) and make sure ... you've asked her about this, you've talked to her about that... Look when women come in here they're in labour and labour is ... an altered state of consciousness.

But an altered state of consciousness is minimised in a system that is predicated on medico-legal anxieties:

The other reason, I think, for that sort of the dominance of that cerebral approach is just the whole anxiety and fear around childbirth which is heavily fuelled by Medico-Legal anxieties, so that there's such a drive to make sure that everything's explained, documented, because if something goes wrong and we haven't done that and we haven't written it in five different places and told the women a thousand times that there is this risk and this risk – that is so powerful... because of the Medico-Legal spectre in private practise people feel very threatened by the possibility of anything going wrong, so the entire decision-making is predicated on, Well Medico-Legally, this just couldn't stand up. Rather than saying, Well what we have to be concerned about is what is clinically or practically best for the woman. It's constantly driven by what would be acceptable in a court of law and hence it becomes a very cerebral thing.

The drive to a 'cerebral' approach, driven by the demands of documentation and accountability—the demands in other words of the bureaucracy—are difficult to resist.

This can also mean that good practice, even safe practice, is not being followed. One of the 'sticking points' identified by Sally was delayed cord clamping. Despite longstanding evidence that delaying cutting of the umbilical cord allows more blood to flow into the baby (and is associated with improved blood iron counts even 6 months later, World Health Organization, 2014), early clamping was one of the practices that Sally found difficult to challenge:

It's funny, there is so much evidence to show that leaving the cord to pulsate is beneficial for the baby on so many levels. What the staff will say is okay, we can let the cord pulse if everything's okay but if there's a problem we're going to need to cut it. It's so difficult to help them to understand that that's when you need to let it pulse... It's not rocket science, but it all comes down to policy. You explain the mechanics behind it, and they say, Oh no, well we can't do it. It's like, Well why not? Oh, that's not policy.

> *Then I try to help them understand that policy isn't law. If the woman is declining the policy that's okay, that they just write that in their notes and that the woman declined. They don't particularly want to go outside their own little square or think outside their square... I think it's a little misguided, that if you... follow the rules nothing bad will happen.*

Protocol allows for dispassion, but often it is passionate care, compassionate care that is needed.

The dispassion of bureaucratic care, the veneer of rationality that it creates, is built upon and reinforces a set of care practices determined not by the woman in front of you but the spectre of culpability and prospective legal entanglements. Here is Sally again, reflecting on how she felt when she was insured as a midwife:

> *I found having insurance makes you practise more defensively than not having it, which is shit because the insurance companies tell you what you can and can't do. Which I can - so I can understand... why the doctors practise that way, because if the insurance company is saying, Well, if you don't do this, this and this and that woman sues you, we won't pay.*

While an Australian professional might be fearful of being sued, the pressures in New Zealand are very different. Litigation has less of a place within the New Zealand health system. The government-funded Accident Compensation Corporation (ACC) pays to cover the costs of ongoing care if there is an accident during birth. Without the insurance companies having quite so much say, the policies that have power are the Standards of Practice produced by the College of Midwives. These standards still step into the room, but many of the New Zealand midwives we interviewed pointed out that part of the approach sanctioned by the College is one that emphasises informed consent and negotiated care. Thus:

> *Rather than being told how to do it ...we would sort of say, Well these are all your options. Then, if [the mother] asks you, What do you think? Then you would certainly state your case... make it quite clear this is what your opinion would be and would be the best practice.... It's up to them to use that information.*

In New Zealand, women we interviewed spoke much less about what they were 'allowed' to do during labour, or about being forced to do something they did not want. Maternal bureaucracies are different in different places.

But at the same time, the established guidelines and protocols for midwifery practice were powerful presences in the birthing rooms of both countries.

EVERYDAY ACTIVISM AND GAMING THE SYSTEM

No matter how powerful the guidelines and policies are, however, there are still openings for a different way of midwifing alongside the demands of the bureaucracy. One strategy that came up commonly in our interviews was the informal 'gaming' of the system; the midwives who formed a scrum to protect me from an episiotomy, the midwives who suggested a 'little walk' to delay hospital admission. These are all little examples of what could be called an 'every day activism' (Chatterton & Pickerill, 2010; Dombroski, 2018). Unlike the protest movement calling for women's rights in childbirth, or the legal cases that test whether a woman has the right to choose where she gives birth, the everyday acts of attentive and compassionate care that occur in spite of what the hierarchy or the protocols might demand, are examples of what Chatterton and Pickerill call 'building the future in the present', and what Kelly Dombroski might consider the activism embedded in everyday care-work (Dombroski, 2018). In these acts caregivers do not just accept that things are as they are. Nor do they jump up and down and demand change. Instead, they simply proceed with providing the care they hope for, in the midst of the mundane everyday circumstances of the system that currently prevails.

In Australia independent midwives are not usually permitted to continue to care as midwives for their women after they have transferred to hospital, so it takes delicacy for a midwife to be able to provide support. Here is Sally again reflecting on how she manages to have such success when she transfers with one of her women into hospital:

It's a very funny dynamic because depending on if the staff members are feeling threatened or not. If they're feeling threatened, the conversation will go something along the lines of, Well Sally, you know you're just a support person here, that you're not making the decisions. Then I'd say that's right, that's absolutely right but this client is…. Generally I'm still trying to be nice to everyone. I'll go in and I set up aromatherapy oils so it's very disarming, because they walk in with that attitude and go, Oh, it smells really nice in here… I don't know why they're so frightened. I just want to work with them. Aren't we all in the same team here?

While New Zealand midwives could point to their standards of practice to explain why they may have 'let' a woman do this or that, in Australia, the space for supporting women to decline advice was harder to find. More midwives spoke about the delicate negotiating skills needed in order to make space for practices that were not the norm, even practices such as allowing for care to be negotiated around the mother's needs and desires. Aromatherapy, a disarming smile, and dogged niceness are some forms of everyday activism, and occasionally it is possible for such everyday actions to be used in support of more systematic change.

This is the case with James, whose position as the head of a busy maternity ward in an affluent Sydney hospital, allows him to use the tools of hierarchy to shift the norms of care in his unit. After speaking at length about the dominance of fear in 'the system', James began to speak also about love. He was telling me about a recent debate in his hospital around the legalities of whether a woman has a right to demand to give birth in the birth centre, or whether she has to do what the hospital tells her if it assesses her to be high-risk and more likely to need emergency intervention:

> *I think we just have to make things very clear and the priority needs to be not about obsessing about whether they're in the birth centre, it's just making sure that whatever space is set up does address the needs of the labouring woman, which is that need to be quiet, the need to be sort of respected, and I think also a prime need for labouring women is the need to be loved.*

A woman who feels loved is a woman who feels safe, cared for, supported. Those emotions are not simply ephemeral or fluffy, they have biochemical imprints which have profound impacts on labour. As I discussed in Chapter 2, normal labour relies upon the body being flooded with the right balance of key hormones (oxytocin, adrenaline, beta-endorphins). The hormones are vital actors in the body's management of pain, and in preparing mother and child for forming attachment of love, and establishing breastfeeding. But the hormones are tricky little things—they respond rapidly to the environment. When stress levels start to rise the balance of hormones changes, slowing down labour, sometimes shutting it off completely.

When James speaks about providing a birth space in which a woman can feel loved, he is talking about being conscious of the mediating role that a woman's carers can have between the biophysical and chemical workings of her body, her own conscious feelings, and the environment she is in—whether the lights are harsh and she's being hassled by the medical staff, whether she needs dim lights and someone to hold her hand, whether her partner is panicking and infecting her with fear; whether the clock is ticking and she is being forced to work to a deadline for labour set by hospital policy, whether she is being faced with the prospect of being transferred from the birth centre to the main ward because of the risk-averse guidelines set more by lawyers than by medical researchers. He is talking about an everyday practice of doctoring and midwifing, that includes not only all these things, but the bureaucratic structures that surround and infuse them. I asked him, 'How do you start talking about love in the context of a hospital?':

> *It's difficult but you don't talk about it I suppose, it's more the way you act towards women, then people sort of get the message. ... some of my younger doctor colleagues might be a bit on edge, as soon as they can see that how powerful it is when someone relates in that loving way to someone then – and particularly if they see that, how it affects the birth – then they take that on board. You don't, yeah actually it's difficult to talk about it and sometimes if you start talking about it, they will back off from that.*
>
> *So again, in reply you know how do we talk about love? We don't talk about it directly, I just say, Well look, it was great the way everyone worked together here. This particular woman... she paid the highest compliment. She didn't know a lot of these people. She knew me, but she said, You worked as a team. I've just said that to everyone and that's how I try to convey that.*

James could almost be citing Annemarie Mol here, and her discussion of the way that doctoring requires working in teams, made up of patient doctor nurse technologies and bodies. Doctoring for Mol requires tinkering, adjusting, balancing out the knowledge and skills with compassion and attentiveness to one person's particular experience and life. But here, doctoring, or midwifing, also requires balancing these things with another dominating yet ephemeral presence in the room—the bureaucracy.

Conclusion

It is one thing to form a strategic alliance with something that is a visible and physical presence in the birth space, but another to hold in mind the invisible presence of regulations and policies. This chapter has drawn on the reflections of midwives, mothers and obstetricians speaking about their negotiations between rigid policy and the more fluid and unpredictable circumstances of giving birth. The policies themselves, and the legal advisors and actuaries who inform policy, the bureaucrats who formalise them, and the managers who police them, are all invisible but powerful presences in the birth space. Their presence can be a challenge for obstetricians, midwives and mothers who are unwilling to blindly follow policy in place of well-informed, empathetic, and responsive practices of care. In many cases, professionals spoke of managing their obligations to bureaucracies by 'playing the game', finding ways to act subversively so as to serve their women well.

The presence of the bureaucracy in the birthing room prompts carers to a quiet response of everyday activism in which values of compassion and persistence must be balanced against the bureaucracy's desire for conformity and formalised accountability. The team at work in the spaces of birth must not only be midwife to the woman in the room, but to the demands and expectations that are carried into the room on the shoulders of midwives and doctors. These are often an uncomfortable blend. There is on the one hand their knowledge of recommended practice, hospital policy, and regulation (what I have been referring to as maternal bureaucracy); and, on the other, their own ethic of care and concern, their gentleness and kindness—what James calls love. Love and bureaucracy do not sit easily together, but, as James suggests, a practice of loving care can balance the protocols and accountability demanded by maternal bureaucracies, with the needs and experience of an individual woman and the particular way her labour unfolds.

REFERENCES

Charlton, B. G. (2010). The cancer of bureaucracy: How it will destroy science, medicine, education; and eventually everything else. *Medical Hypotheses, 74*(6), 961–965. https://doi.org/10.1016/j.mehy.2009.11.038.

Chatterton, P., & Pickerill, J. (2010). Everyday activism and transitions towards post-capitalist worlds. *Transactions of the Institute of British Geographers, 35*(4), 475–490.

Dombroski, K. (2018). Learning to be affected: Maternal connection, intuition and "elimination communication". *Emotion, Space and Society, 26,* 72–79. https://doi.org/10.1016/j.emospa.2017.09.004.

Eastman, K. S., & Loustaunau, M. O. (1988). Reacting to the medical bureaucracy: Lay midwifery as a birthing alternative. *Marriage & Family Review, 11*(3–4), 23–37. https://doi.org/10.1300/J002v11n03_03.

Hoag, C. (2011). Assembling partial perspectives: Thoughts on the anthropology of bureaucracy. *Political and Legal Anthropology Critical Review, 34*(1), 81–94.

Mol, A. (2008). *The logic of care: Health and the problem of patient choice.* London and New York: Routledge.

World Health Organization. (2014). *Delayed umbilical cord clamping for improved maternal and infant health and nutrition outcomes—Guideline.* https://www.who.int/nutrition/publications/guidelines/cord_clamping/en/.

CHAPTER 6

Loving Technologies

Abstract This chapter turns to the role of technology in defining modern birth and particularly the role of the foetal heart rate monitor (Cardiotocogram or CTG) that has come to be relied upon as an indication of the baby's wellbeing. The medical technologies of modern obstetrics are often assumed to be allied with practices of 'medical birth', that is, birthing care focused on: providing a 'safe' birth that avoids unnecessary 'risks', close monitoring of mother and foetus, and unhesitating introduction of technological solutions to a difficult labour. This chapter explores how such technologies are caught up in a more complex assemblage of care. How would obstetric technologies be understood if positioned among multiple actors (human and non-human) that contribute to shaping wellbeing at the beginning of life? How do CTGs and scalpels engage in the relations and practices of 'caring-with' childbirth? The practice of caring can unfold *with* rather than being led by, or opposed to, the machines with whom we share the birth space.

Keywords Technology · Machinic agency · Caring-with · Ethical negotiation

My midwife was reluctant when she asked my permission. I try not to use it, she said, but we need to know how baby is doing. She'd been stuck in that birth canal for 2 hours and they wanted to know if she was in distress. So in they

© The Author(s) 2020
K. McKinnon, *Birthing Work*,
https://doi.org/10.1007/978-981-15-0010-7_6

went to hook a wire through the top of her scalp, poor dear. The wire connected to a monitor which amplified her heartbeat for us all to hear—was she still calm and steady? Was she panicking? The rhythm of her heart would tell. But the rhythm was not steady, it came and went and sometimes disappeared altogether. Somehow I didn't find that at all concerning, maybe I just 'knew' that she was ok, as women sometimes say they 'just know'. My mother, on the other hand, standing by the bed and trying to muster her courage, heard the intermittent audio and understood the child to be in trouble. It had been a long second stage. All the while my baby lingered on the doorstep of life, and my mother worried.

It did not feel that way to me, but my child and I were hovering at that ambiguous point where life and death perch at the ready, and one can slip either way. For centuries childbirth has been like this—one of the most dangerous moments in a woman's life, with no guarantee that things will go well, that mother and child will make it through to live and thrive.

In that well-appointed hospital room, I was not near death, and nor was my child as it turns out. This was nothing to do with the suite of medical technologies on hand. The midwife, reluctant to hurt an unborn babe, had been too gentle with attaching the wire and it had not gone in securely enough. The heartbeat wavered not because my daughter's heart was weakening, but because the electrode was giving a shaky signal. I knew this and was not concerned. And sure enough when she slipped out she was a bit blue and a bit squashed, and was most certainly upset at having been first squeezed and then impaled on her way out, but her cry was hearty (it let us all know how she was feeling and she has been pretty good at letting us know ever since).

The foetal scalp electrode that was attached to my daughter is just one of the many hi-tech devices employed in the practice of childbirth. My 'knowing' that everything was fine was in sharp contrast to the anxiety produced for my mother by what she took to be the accurate information broadcast by the machine. Our contrasting experiences in that room point to the very different ways that machinic partners-in-care do their work with us in the birthing suite: they are meant to tell us what is really going on, but reality is often more ambiguous.

There is a great deal of very sophisticated technology deployed in a contemporary hospital birth suite: scanners and monitors of various kinds, various concoctions and the implements that deliver them intravenously, go-go gadget beds, and bottles of compressed oxygen are just some. The piece of equipment that dominates most delivery rooms, however, is the

Cardiotocogram (CTG), that monitors the baby's heart rate. In every hospital room that our respondents worked in, the CTG was there. Jane, a midwife trained in the UK and working in a New Zealand hospital, talked at length about the demands of the CTG: It's big, '*loud and noisy*', it rolls on wheels, and alongside the bed, '*takes pride of place*'. When a woman arrives, bringing the machine out and attaching a woman to it, is the first thing that is done:

> *Well, if a woman comes into us in labour, any kind of reason that she will come to us, she might just have a bit of pain, the first thing we do is a CTG. So, to assess to the baby's wellbeing and that's the big machine. So the first thing we will do is, Hi, how are you doing? Down you go on the bed and put the machine on. So that's the routine and there is a body of evidence to say that if someone is low risk, we don't have to do a CTG, particularly if a woman is in early labour but within that hospital environment, because you are in that space, it's staring at you and I think people just go Yeah, I will do it. It's that sort of reassurance... by its very presence it's saying, use me!*

Within the hospital environment the CTG (rather like the bed discussed in Chapter 4) *calls* us to it. It is, in that environment, identifiable as part of the coalition of actors who assemble for a medical birth. It is accompanied, always, by the presence of harsh bright lights, ready access to IV, epidurals, scalpels, and the professionals trained to wield them.

The CTG is also a notable *absence* from the space of homebirth, where it is enough to check the baby's wellbeing with the periodic use of a handheld heart rate monitor or to listen through a cone-like Pinard. For many, the CTG exists in opposition to a natural birth. As one mother, Melanie, noted, the machinery just '*didn't feel organic*'. Davis-Floyd and Davis (1996) argue that the presence of the CTG is a sign of the 'technocratic model' of birth that has come to dominate birthing care. The technocratic model sees women framed as defective machines who must be 'hooked up to other, more perfect diagnostic machines' in order to make sure that birth will be 'better' (Davis-Floyd & Davis, 1996, p. 238):

> Under this model, authoritative knowledge – the knowledge on the basis of which decisions are made and actions are taken… is vested in these machines and those who know how to manipulate and interpret them.

By investing our trust in the knowledge of the machines (in place of a woman's inner experience and the embodied intuitive knowledge of a midwife) we are, Davis-Floyd claims, making the mistake of valuing the 'machine-like' processes of conscious deductive reasoning above and beyond processes of creative intuition. For Davis-Floyd, this overvaluing of the rational is indicative of the 'technocratic model of reality' that dominates western societies, and is the hallmark of a masculine patriarchal society fundamentally opposed to womanhood:

> that model guarantees [all women] continued psychological disempowerment by the everyday constructs of the culture-at-large, and her alienation both from political power *and* from the physiological attributes of womanhood. (Davis-Floyd, 2003, p. 291, emphasis original)

Davis-Floyd demonstrates an important commitment to the value of womanhood and the worth of, perhaps, a more maternal rationality (that she calls intuition). Yet, given that the machine is in our birth spaces and unlikely to abandon them, I explore in this chapter how we might form a different kind of relationship to that beige beast in the corner of the room.

I work with some conceptual clues provided by scholars in the field of human geography. One is Levi Bryant, whose idea of 'onto-cartography' is helpful to rethink the relationships between humans and machines (Bryant, 2014). Bryant's reading of theorists Giles Deleuze and Félix Guattari provides a view into the way machinic-being is intimately linked with human-being. He suggests that rather than seeing machines as something dead and disconnected from us, in fact, connectedness is part of what a machine *is* and what it *does*. I also work with the inspiration of geographers J. K. Gibson-Graham, Jenny Cameron, and Stephen Healy (2013) whose work on ethical negotiations provides an exemplar for how we might manage our shared being with the machine.[1] They provide a pathway based on recognising sociality in the midst of economic relationships and interactions which might at first appear cold and rational. Building on these resources I wonder if even the unyielding operations of something made of metal and plastic can be negotiated with and enrolled to support, rather than negate, what Davis-Floyd and Davis call 'the whole of birth – its rhythms,

---

[1] An additional, and important inspiration in this chapter is the work of Donna Haraway, who has long explored the fluid boundaries between humans and our non-human companions in the world (Haraway, 1990, 2008). I do not discuss her work directly, but the curiosity about how we might thinking differently about our machinic companions in the birth space owes a debt to her work.

its juiciness, its intense sexuality, fluidity, ecstasy and pain' (Davis-Floyd & Davis 1996, p. 239).

In this chapter I use these clues as I reflect on the experiences shared by midwives and mothers about the use of the CTG. In so doing, I am curious about what can be learned about how machines work alongside us in the birth space; whether it is possible to think about machines who care; and whether machines have to be aligned always with a technocratic birth. This chapter considers how the CTG, among other birth technologies, does caring work *with* us in the birth space.

THE CONTROVERSIAL HISTORY OF THE CTG

The technology employed in the birthing room is supposed to be one of the things that buffers us from the appalling maternal morbidity rates of the past. In Australia in 1875, for every 100,000 living babies born, 643 women died. In 2016 the rate was 8.5 per 100,000 (AIHW, 2018). But even now, there are places where it is no safer than it was for Australian women in 1875: in the Congo it was 693 per 100,000 in 2015 (WHO, UNICEF, UNFPA, World Bank Group, & United Nations Population Division, 2015), even within Australia, rates of maternal morbidity for Aboriginal and Torres Strait Islanders are double that of the rest of the population (AIHW, 2015). While birth is a universal human experience, its risks are not experienced universally. With many other mothers whose experiences with the machines of birth were not positive, I have a hard time not feeling hostile to the CTG and the technocratic take-over that it represents. My sympathies are with Davis-Floyd. However, the CTG was not born of efforts to take birth away from mothers, but to ensure fewer mothers and babes died during the process.

The CTG, or Cardiotocogram, was designed to allow birth attendants to monitor the heart rate of the unborn infant. The precursors of the CTG include the stethograph, invented in 1816 by René Laennec (Saling & Dräger, 2014) at a time when little was known about what foetal heart rates could reveal about the health of the baby or the likelihood of a live birth. It was difficult to distinguish the baby's heart rate from the mother's, especially during contractions (and this remains a problem with modern electronic Doppler instruments), but in 1876 French obstetrician Adolph Pinard developed the first stethoscope designed particularly for listening to the child's heartbeat (Pettker & Campbell, 2012). The wooden (or sometimes plastic or stainless steel) cone-shaped implement, the Pinard horn, remains in wide usage, and is considered by many to be a more reliable, as well as less intrusive and incontrovertibly harmless, way to monitor foetal heart rates.

Since the discovery that 'the activity of the heart is based on electric processes' by Carlo Matteucci in 1843,[2] there was experimentation with different approaches to using an electrocardiogram to monitor heart rates (Saling & Dräger, 2014). The first prototype of the modern CTG scanners was a 6-foot-high machine built by Orvan Walter Hess and Edward Hon in 1957. Two later innovations made possible the routine use of electronic monitoring. One was Edward Hon's innovation of using a 'clip' electrode fastened to the infant's scalp (which is actually much like a miniature corkscrew). The other was the work to create portable cardiotocograph machines, the first on the market released by Hewlett Packard in 1969 (Saling & Dräger, 2014).

The CTG, and other Electronic Foetal Monitoring (EFM) technologies, are now a ubiquitous presence in many hospital maternity wards. Sartwelle (2012) reports that 'approximately 85% of the 4,000,000 annual births [in the USA] are EFM monitored' (p. 313). But its routine use is controversial. The appeal of the CTG is apparent—it gives birth attendants a view into the body and an indication of foetal wellbeing during labour. Dr Joshua Copel, a professor of obstetrics, gynaecology and paediatrics at the Yale University School of Medicine, says 'Before these monitors were invented, the uterus was literally a black box... we knew the babies were in there, and they came out' (Baranauckas, 2002).

However, the attempt to constantly look inside the 'black box' has effects.

Several systematic reviews have found that there is limited utility in having a constant information feed of an infant's heart rate, and that there are marginal benefits to neonatal health. Sartwelle (2012) is one of the most scathing critics of routine EFM:

> It's scientific foundation is feeble; inter-observer/intra-observer reliability is poor; the false-positive prediction of foetal distress rate is greater than 99%; it

---

[2] One of the first successful applications of this technology for pregnancy was the foetal electrocardiogram used by Cremer in 1906 to create separate recordings of the mother's and the infant's heartbeat. This was achieved by applying 'special electrolytic chlorinated silver electrodes', one to the mother's abdomen and the other inserted in the vagina (Saling & Dräger, 2014, p. 8).

has substantially increased the caesarean section rate with attendant mortality and morbidity; and it failed completely in its initial stated promise—reducing by half the incidence of cerebral palsy (CP), mental retardation (MR), and peri-natal mortality. (pp. 313–314)

Sartwelle charts the emergence of routine scans as a practice built on 'unverified nineteenth-century speculation about the meaning of variations in foetal heartbeats' (p. 319). The parameters for diagnosing foetal distress remain based on a study conducted in *1893*, and not since replicated or verified (Saling & Dräger, 2014). Upon this foundation twentieth-century researchers sought better techniques for accurately measuring heartbeats, published papers that seemed to cement the speculative connections being made between abnormally slow heartbeats, foetal distress, lack of oxygen and brain damage, and, according to Sartwelle, allowed obstetric medicine to be 'hypnotized by the lure of gadgets, quick fixes, and simple cures to complex problems as was the rest of American society' (p. 320).

Sartwelle is not alone in his suspicions. EFM was supposed to allow an accurate way to monitor foetal wellbeing, providing birth attendants with a clear indication of whether they must intervene. What numerous randomised trials have shown, however, is that this is not what is happening. In fact the evidence appears to show, overwhelmingly, that electronic foetal monitoring has little or no beneficial impact on birth outcomes, leading the Royal College of Midwives, and the Royal College of Obstetricians and Gynaecologists in the UK to issue a joint statement that EFM 'is not routinely recommended for healthy women at low risk of complications in established labour' (Royal College of Midwives, 2017). Now there is concern that routine use of the CTG is contributing the increasing rate of unnecessary caesareans (Paterno, McElroy, & Regan, 2016). Clark and Hankins (2003) argue that the continued routine use of it is therefore absurd:

a test leading to an unnecessary major abdominal operation in more than 99.5% of cases should be regarded by the medical community as absurd at best… Operative intervention based on electric foetal monitoring has probably done more harm than good. (p. 631)

All this leaves us with the question, if the CTG does not predict foetal distress and allow action to be taken preventing brain damage, what *does* it do?

The CTG Is a Witness

One of the key reasons for routine use of the CTG appears to be that it is an excellent way to create an ongoing record of foetal heartbeat, thus creating a document that can serve as legal evidence. This fact is clear from the script of a nurses training video designed to introduce trainee nurses and midwives to the appropriate use of EFM. After a woman is admitted and has been given a hospital gown to wear, the video tells its student viewers, you must attach them to the electronic monitoring device:

> The monitor tracing or its electronic counterpart is a legal part of the patient's medical records, as such it should include identifying information and times and events related to the patient's care. The nurse identifies non-reassuring tracings and is responsible for initiating appropriate nursing actions and for notifying a physician. Once the nurse notifies the physician, a timely response should be expected. (Medcom, 2008)

The 'trace'—a printout of the heart rate—has become evidence for what can be construed as *un*timely responses to danger signs. If something goes wrong, the trace can be consulted to determine whether someone failed to pick up on warning signs and act appropriately. What it is that the trace actually shows, however, and whether or not what is indicated is indeed distress, is unclear. Sartwelle argues that the machine is not there in the corner of the birthing suite to protect the unborn child, and enable 'correct' decisions in care, it is there as 'an unscientific legal prophylactic'. (Sartwelle, 2012, p. 324)

Sartwelle's diagnosis rang true in the experience of the midwives we interviewed in this research. Jane for instance, the midwife we met at hte bginning of this chapter, told me that while the protocols are in place to *not* use the CTG for a woman with a low-risk pregnancy:

> *it's quite difficult to defend your practice if you don't want to do one. It's quite difficult to and the fact of the matter is it's there. If you do it and it is fine you have covered your butt type of thing.*

The CTG is a 'butt-coverer'. It is there as a record keeper. It is there to assist in the practice of defensive medicine and to stand as witness in case a mother should turn litigant, and obstetricians and midwives turn defendants.

THE MACHINE IS A WORKER

As well as being a legal record the CTG is, like many modern machines, a labour-saving device. In the emotionally charged space of the birthing room the presence of the CTG is reassuringly unwavering. It is unaffected by the lateness of the hour or lack of sleep, it does not get grumpy or emotional (although the professional interpreting the trace may be affected by all of these things). What the unresting machine does, however, is to make it possible for one human being (with all her needs for sleep and rest and food) to monitor several women at once. Having taken-for-granted the 'fact' that foetal heart rate is the best way to know how well the baby is doing, and once a machine was able to perform that task, a midwife was no longer needed to sit with a mother and intuit her way into the 'black box' of the uterus. Suddenly one midwife could care for several women at once, providing a massive increase in the efficiency (if not the effectiveness) of the maternity ward.

The efficiency of the hospital is experienced by every mother that mentioned it as being 'left alone'. For some, this was a good thing, seen less as being mediated by a machine than as an indication of the knowledge and experience of the carers. Melanie was one such mother. She gave birth in a hospital on the north shore of Sydney where the midwives spent little time with her through her labours. She remarked that:

what's so beautiful about experienced midwives is that assessment comes at a glance. They will just look at a labouring woman and say, She's right... So to have somebody walk into the room, look at me, turn up the machine and walk out, I didn't feel unsupported by that.

Some mothers, in contrast, found that being left without the guidance of a midwife was difficult and upsetting. Wendy did not dwell on the fact that her midwives were not present with her, but the effect was a feeling of being abandoned:

They left me alone a lot and I think it was because I had a doula as well. But then I think they leave you alone a lot anyway because they've got other things to do. But yeah, I didn't get any support.

The machine, though it may be the one relied upon to monitor the mother and the baby, cannot exude empathy or a feeling of loving care. It does however, provide a view inside the 'black box' of the womb not just for an attentive midwife or a mother attuned to her own body, but to the many others who may be present.

THE REASSURING INSISTENCE OF THE CTG

For many midwives, doctors, mothers and the family members that were supporting them, the CTG was what they turned to for knowledge of what was going on. Kate's experience is one example of this. She had high blood pressure towards the end of her first pregnancy, a risk sign for the potentially life-threatening condition of pre-eclampsia. As a result, her first baby was induced:

> *Well they gave me the gel at night and then nothing happened. Then in the morning my blood pressure was really, really high so they're like, Right, we're not doing the gel again, the baby's coming out now. So then they broke my waters and moved me to a delivery room.*

In that room with her there were 'five or six medical students and the doctor and the midwives' to witness her waters being broken, then she was given a drip and connected to the CTG machine.

> *At the time, Jo was panicking because the midwife explained to him what the CTG and – 'Don't worry about the numbers, we only have to worry if it drops down to this'. He's just looking at the thing the whole time. Then it dropped down to that and he's just like, ahh!*

It is understandable that Jo should have turned to the machine for understanding: where the movements and noises of labour are unfamiliar, the machine is producing a view inside the 'black box' that is legible to anyone who is familiar with machines and knows how to read a graph.

For some women, the machine offers reassurance that they feel they can depend on. In the midst of a long and difficult birth, especially for a woman giving birth for the first time, this insight into the rhythm of the child's heartbeat can be encouraging. This was Hannah's experience:

> *The good thing was every time they monitored her heartbeat she was just totally chilled, which was very reassuring. But yeah, I think at some point I'd maybe started to think maybe this baby will never be born [laughs]. So when she was born, and she was healthy and wriggling and that was just very fantastic.*

Mediated by technology, the child has a way to speak to us that we know how to hear, and that can be reassuring. Conversely, Davis-Floyd might say that what this means is that we've forgotten how to listen to the body speak in its own ways.

TECHNOLOGICAL RELATIONSHIPS: WITH OURSELVES, EACH OTHER AND THE MACHINE

Davis-Floyd and Davis are concerned that what the CTG does, when it is relied upon as the only view into the black box of labour, is to disconnect women from 'their natural bodies' and the experience of 'the whole of birth' (1996, p. 239). These scholars are concerned that women, and midwives, are losing the ability to intuit or to value the deeply embodied knowledge that is important to holistic care. For Davis-Floyd and Davis, the ubiquitous presence of the machine is imposing an increasing separation—of women from their own bodies and of midwives from their empathetic knowledges and the skill of intuition that comes from long experience:

> The trustworthiness of intuition is intrinsically related to its emergence from that matrix of physical, emotional, and spiritual connection – a matrix that gives intuition more power and credibility, in these midwives' eyes, than the information that arises from the *technologies of separation*. (p. 260, my emphasis)

This sense of separation was certainly reflected in some of the stories we were told. For some women the only close contact they had with hospital midwives was when they tried to apply a monitor of some kind. Laura (whose story I discussed in Chapter 5) related how, in her experience, the machine seemed to be called upon to attend to her in the place of human care:

> *Midwives would come in with a couple of students and congregate at the end of the bed, really. There was very little interaction with me physically apart from attempting to get a [trace] from me.*

Daily life in much of the (post-industrial, urbanised) world is lived alongside machines, and we are used to machines telling us the time, telling us the weather, telling us how fast we are going and how far we have to go. We turn to the machine to give us a measure of life, but in doing so (and as

Davis-Floyd suggests) we perhaps turn away from attending to embodied experience and knowledge.

Melanie, who spoke about 'assessment at a glance' above, and who did not seem to mind, also expressed reservations about what the CTG was doing to her birth experience. While it was ok for the professionals to consult it, she reflected that it interfered with her own apprehension of the embodied experience of labour:

> *I had to stop looking at it because I was using it as an indicator of what was going on. I think they actually had to recalibrate it because it started to get really full on and it's like, Okay, we are going to change it now, because it has been working in these perimeters and now, like that's off the scale. Just knowing all of that is quite odd I think, having that mechanical input and then a mechanical feedback.*
>
> *So, I had to stop looking at it because I was using it as a measure of how strong the experience was and that was uncomfortable I think in hindsight. I stopped looking at it and I think it went better from then.*

Like many other mothers and carers and birth attendants, Melanie looked to the machine to tell her how the labour was going. In her case she was confronted by the knowledge that the machine did not operate as an independent and neutral barometer for childbirth—the awareness that a machine is flawed, that it carries the marks of the life it has lived, is antithetical to the role of tireless reliability that we ask it to perform. Like any machine, however, the CTG sometimes breaks down, and it relies upon its human colleagues to not only interpret and act upon the information it gathers, but to repair and recalibrate it.

Reliance on a (flawed) technological intermediary can also have the effect of alienating a woman from her own embodied experience of labour. And that alienation is not just spontaneous. It is imposed, sometimes quite forcefully, by the coalition of what Davis-Floyd calls technocratic birth. In the same way that a bed can become a prison (as discussed in Chapter 4) the CTG machine can become the jailer.

For Trish the birth of her second child was particularly intense. The intensity of the contractions was overwhelming and as she recalled the experience, she remembered feeling 'totally out of control'. In this state she encountered a midwife who insisted that she submit to being strapped on the CTG:

> *I got really angry at her and I can remember that moment. I can't remember much else. … She strapped me up and made me lie down. She made me lie down to do it, and I said, No, I'm not lying down, get me up. I had to fight her to get up. They don't have to strap you down, they've got a mobile machine.*

Her memories of the room in which she gave birth do not exist beyond the boundaries of that bed that she was strapped onto:

> *I don't remember the room. I can remember being on the bed. I can remember being angry about trying to want to stand up.*

While Davis-Floyd helps us see how birth technologies disconnect mothers and midwives from the experience of birth, applying Bryant's (2014) definition of a machine brings up some other possibilities.

For Bryant a machine by definition takes one thing or things (input) and transforms that into something else (the product). A CTG takes electronic signals through the flesh of a baby, the amniotic fluid, and the boundary of a mother's womb and abdomen. It tidies up the messy signal and transforms them into a singular message—the trace. Because it is busy with something coming in (messy electrical inputs) and something going out (the product or 'trace'), the machine is necessarily bound up in a relationship—it exists only in and through relationships with the babies it measures, and the nurses and midwives and obstetricians and lawyers and judges and expert witnesses and mothers (and nervous grandmothers) who read and listen to the traces it produces. The traces that are produced in turn cause something else to happen: the midwife to call the obstetrician, the obstetrician to pull out her forceps, the grandmother to worry and so on. The CTG needs there to be an infant heart beating, and it needs there to be someone listening and acting according to what it says—*it needs to be connected.*

Understanding the machine as existing only in and through its connections to others offers a challenge to the assumption that birth technologies necessarily separate and isolate, that technologies deconstruct birth and deny the value of connection. Perhaps the issue is not that they cause disconnection, but that they enable a different kind of connection.

Narratives of the Pinard, for example, posit its use in alliance with natural and unobtrusive, more *organic* birth-care. It is quiet, it does not emit electromagnetic signals, and somehow these qualities see it placed in affinity with an understanding of the sacredness of birth. But in the nineteenth century, the Pinard horn was the pinnacle of new technology in obstetrics.

In their time, so too were the Jizo statues and the Babylonian incantations that sought to guide mother and child through the dangers of childbirth. As objects made by human creativity, through expert skill and craftsmanship, and with a care for the (beautiful) precision required to engineer them, each of these things is not exclusively an object of technology, material culture, or magic. The magical properties of the CTG are no less spiritual for being mediated by electricity. Witness the wonder on a child's face the first time she hears her own heartbeat through a toy stethoscope. Witness the tears on a mother's face on hearing the heartbeat of her unborn child for the first time. These experiences remain profound, and sacred, all for being mediated by tools of scientific technologies.

What all these things have in common is what they *do*. What they do is to help us connect—as birthing women connecting with ourselves, our unborn babies, our spiritual guides and the unfolding arrival of a child into the world. Viewed through the conceptual language of Deleuze and Guattari (1987; as discussed by Bryant, 2014) all of these things could be seen as machines. They are techno-spiritual artefacts that perform a function, they take what we bring to them and produce something different with it: The Pinard horn renders heartbeat into listenable sound, the incantation enables the protection and guidance of the deities, the mandala creates focus and calm, the CTG renders electric signals in spidery graphs. Through the function they perform we can also see how each of these techno-spiritual artefacts is present in a network of productive relationships—relationships that must be negotiated.

Negotiating with (and Around) the Machine

Negotiation is, according to midwife and doula trainer Susan Ross, one of the primary responsibilities of a birth attendant, and especially the role of the doula whose job it is to act as both carer and advocate for a birthing woman. Ross recalls one incident when she was supporting a woman who had to transfer from a birth centre to the hospital delivery suite. The mother had been very clear about not wanting a foetal scalp electrode to be used, but the midwife was placing her under pressure to accept one. They were using a CTG with a belt around her belly, but the monitor was showing that the baby's heart rate was dropping:

> So the very, very young midwife said, Oh look, they're in distress, like this. So, I gently pointed out that I thought it was probably loss of contact. It just means

that when a woman's in an awkward position – not lying flat on her back on her bed very still so that they can get a good trace … So [the midwife said] we're just going to pop in a little clip. The mum looked at me. I said, so she's talking about a scalp electrode …The mother was leaning over the bed and the midwife was almost screaming, saying foetal distress. The mum looked up and she said actually, my baby's fine.

And she was right. Ross negotiated with two registrar doctors, a resident doctor, an anaesthetist and a midwife to not use the scalp electrode, and as a result it was 'hugely empowering' for a woman whose hopes for a natural birth in a birth centre had had to be abandoned.

When we work with machines there is the possibility to encounter others, and ourselves, in ways very different to the encounters possible in a completely 'natural' birth. Yet there is also room to shape how we encounter others through, and resulting from, those technologically mediated encounters. The machinic presence of the CTG takes an input (the electric signal), transforms it into something else (the 'trace'), and in doing so causes other action to take place. In that web of input and output there is no guarantee what the result will look like—it differs every time. The way that it differs is interpreted in some settings as a failure, i.e. the CTG fails to be reliable because the interpretation of its messages depends on the subjective understanding of the doctor. But from a different point of view what this actually means is that the machine is no more perfect than we are. What we make happen when we use the CTG is down to how the machine and the human negotiate our being together.

In their work to elaborate strategies for transforming our communities, Gibson-Graham et al. (2013) offer a vision for what negotiating being-together can look like. Gibson-Graham et al. focus their analytical attention on the operations of the economy. In *Take Back The Economy* they draw our attention to the diverse transactions through which we secure the goods and services that we need. Drawing what they call a 'distant others dandelion', Gibson-Graham et al. point out that through each of these transactions we become connected to the chain of producers and distributors of that good: the phone we choose to buy connects us to the workers in China that made it, the t-shirt we pick up at an op-shop connects us to the person who donated it, the carrot we buy from the cooperative connects us to the farmer that grew it. Each of these transactions can be analysed for how it fits with our values. For Gibson-Graham et al., they are most interested in understanding whether the way we purchase our goods and services meets the criteria for 'ethical interconnections': that is, interconnections that benefit people and planet, that do less harm and more good. As we become more aware of the ethical implications of our purchasing decisions, it becomes possible to negotiate towards decisions that better accord with the ethical concerns we hold dear. There is nothing hard and fast about the idea of an ethical negotiation, there are no firm rules or set trajectories. There are not even concrete goals, except perhaps to endeavour to act in ways that foster what we cherish.

Likewise the very thing that concerns so many medical researchers about the routine use of the CTG in the delivery room is the thing that leaves it open to the possibility of ethical negotiation. Rather than assuming that we ought to always know what the CTG is telling us and what the 'right' response ought to be, our techno-machinic communications can, and do, bend. When we let them bend, and we shape that movement around what is important (the avoidance of the unnecessary harm of a pierced scalp, or the disempowerment of a mother who wants a lotus birth), then the practice of caring can unfold *with* rather than being led by, or opposed to, the machines with whom we share the birth space.

The following story tell us how this might look in the practice of, as the respondent states, 'good obstetrics' and more generally good care. Emily, a senior midwife in New Zealand told this story:

> *I recently had a woman who I took in for a CTG tracing because she was post-dates and while we were doing the tracing she had this enormous deceleration. And she was planning a home birth. She'd done calm birth. She was really ready for something; a beautiful birth and she had to go to a caesarean within six or seven minutes of this bradycardia. I was in shock.*
>
> *Her husband came in. He was ready to defend her right to not have a caesarean and take battle with the obstetrician. The obstetrician stayed very calm and he explained why we couldn't wait, and it was cord compression and that it was a really severe emergency. The husband looked at me and I went, we don't have an option, and that obstetrician really held the space. He held the guy's anger, his attack for being a doctor and wanting a caesarean. He held all of that and yet was really rational about the way he dealt with him and he was really generous and kind about the way he dealt with that....*
>
> *I thought, Oh thank God, because he could've actually said, okay have your dead baby if you want [laughs], out the door, or been quite rude back. But actually, he was really skilled, and when you work with people that operate like that, it's like, Phew. That's when we've got really good obstetrics.*

So I went back to see him to say ...They want a lotus birth. Is there any reason why you have to cut the cord? And he said, no because he was really wanting this baby out. So we had [the lotus birth] in theatre... and kept the placenta attached, with all the theatre staff going, 'I've never seen that before. It's really crazy'. So, what he did was he allowed them to maintain some integrity in terms of their birth plan by doing that; which was just fantastic.

In this story the CTG does its job well. Calling to the midwife and the obstetrician to attend to a massive deceleration in the baby's heart rate, it spurs them into action. But this action does not need to carry through the cold-heartedness of the machine. And, surely, there is no necessity either, for our communication with the machine to cancel out our spirit or love.

CONCLUSION

One of the fiercest areas of argument in the 'birth wars' is the role of technology in the birthing room and the ways in which a technocratic model has displaced women-centred care. This chapter has explored the role of technology in defining modern birth, particularly the role of the foetal heart rate monitor that has come to be relied upon as an indication of the baby's wellbeing. The medical technologies of modern obstetrics are often assumed to be allied with practices of 'medical birth', that is, birthing care focused on providing a 'safe' birth that avoids unnecessary 'risks', close monitoring of mother and foetus, and unhesitating introduction of technological solutions to a difficult labour.

I have argued in this chapter that such technologies are caught up in a more complex set of relationships. Our connections with machines are available to ethical negotiation, opening up more productive ways to encounter obstetric technology across the 'natural' vs 'medical' divide. The CTG is just one party to the negotiations around how the childbirth will unfold. The stories recounted here highlight how the CTG's record of foetal heartbeat can be placed alongside the obstetrician's concern for safety, the parents desire for a gentle birth, and the midwife's duty to be with the woman. Such interrelationships may be technologically mediated, they may lack 'juiciness', but they are no less social for all that. And as they are social, they are also subject to values and ethics that govern social relations. Likewise, the very thing that concerns so many medical researchers about the routine use of the CTG in the delivery room is the thing that leaves it open to the possibility of ethical negotiation. Rather than assuming that we ought to always know what the CTG is telling us and what the 'right' response ought to be, our techno-machinic communications can, and do, bend.

These stories show us that even in the moment of saving a baby's life, it is possible to shape care around what is important to a woman: The machine does not have to insist that we pierce a babies scalp, force a mother to lie on the bed, or disempower a mother who wants a lotus birth. Rather than abandon loving-care in response to the call of the machine, there is space to communicate and connect. The work of care can unfold *with*, rather than being led by, or opposed to, the machines with whom we share the birth space.

REFERENCES

AIHW. (2015). *Maternal deaths low in Australia, but indigenous women remain at greater risk*. Retrieved June 5, 2017, from Australian Institute of Health and Welfare Media Releases website: http://www.aihw.gov.au/media-release-detail/?id=60129551418.

AIHW. (2018). *Maternal deaths in Australia 2016*. Retrieved from Australian Institute of Health and Welfare website: https://www.aihw.gov.au/reports/mothers-babies/maternal-deaths-in-australia-2016/contents/report.

Baranauckas, C. (2002). Dr. Orvan W. Hess, 96, Dies; Developed fetal heart monitor. *The New York Times*. Retrieved from https://www.nytimes.com/2002/09/16/us/dr-orvan-w-hess-96-dies-developed-fetal-heart-monitor.html.

Bryant, L. R. (2014). *Onto-cartography: An ontology of machines and media*. Edinburgh: Edinburgh University Press.

Clark, S. L., & Hankins, G. D. V. (2003). Temporal and demographic trends in cerebral palsy—Fact and fiction. *American Journal of Obstetrics and Gynecology, 188*(3), 628–633. https://doi.org/10.1067/mob.2003.204.

Davis-Floyd, R. (2003). *Birth as an American rite of passage*. Berkeley: University of California Press.

Davis-Floyd, R., & Davis, E. (1996). Intuition as authoritative knowledge in midwifery and homebirth. *Medical Anthropology Quarterly, 10*(2), 237–269. https://doi.org/10.1525/maq.1996.10.2.02a00080.

Deleuze, G., & Guattari, F. (1987). *A thousand plateaus: Capitalism and schizophrenia*. Minneapolis: University of Minnesota Press.

Gibson-Graham, J. K., Cameron, J., & Healy, S. (2013). *Take back the economy*. Minneapolis: University of Minnesota Press.

Goddard, R. (2001, June). Electronic fetal monitoring is not necessary for low risk labours. *BMJ, 322*(June), 1436–1437.

Haraway, D. (1990). *Simians, cyborgs, and women: The reinvention of nature.* New York: Routledge.

Haraway, D. (2008). Companion species, mis-recognition, and queer worlding. In N. Giffney & M. J. Hird (Eds.), *Queering the non/human.* Aldershot: Ashgate.

Medcom. (2008). *Obstetrical nursing, electronic fetal monitoring.* Cypress, CA: Medcom.

Paterno, M. T., McElroy, K., & Regan, M. (2016). Electronic fetal monitoring and cesarean birth: A scoping review. *Birth, 43*(4), 277–284. https://doi.org/10.1111/birt.12247.

Pettker, C. M., & Campbell, K. H. (2012). Antepartum fetal assessment. In C. A. Gleason & S. U. Devaskar (Eds.), *Avery's diseases of the newborn* (9th ed., pp. 129–139). https://doi.org/10.1016/B978-1-4377-0134-0.10013-7.

Royal College of Midwives. (2017). RCM and RCOG publish joint statement on electronic fetal monitoring. *RCM.* Retrieved February 23, 2019, from https://www.rcm.org.uk/news-views-and-analysis/news/rcm-and-rcog-publish-joint-statement-on-electronic-fetal-monitoring.

Saling, E., & Dräger, M. (2014). Fetal heart rate activity and measurements of labor activity. In *The beginnings of perinatal medicine* (pp. 5–21). Munich, Germany and Boston, MA: De Gruyter.

Sartwelle, T. (2012). Electronic fetal monitoring: A bridge too far. *Journal of Legal Medicine, 33*(3), 313–379.

WHO, UNICEF, UNFPA, World Bank Group, & United Nations Population Division. (2015). *Trends in maternal mortality: 1990 to 2015.* https://www.who.int/reproductivehealth/publications/monitoring/maternal-mortality-2015/en/.

CHAPTER 7

Taking Time

Abstract In the birth space our interviews highlighted the pressures of time, and how the clock regulated and policed their labours. Time has come to govern labour and the clock has come to have a ubiquitous presence in most labour wards. It is the clock and its relentless marking of time that comes to the fore in the hospital labouring room, where the calibrated measurement of time has an affinity with an institution dominated by technologies of measurement, and a workplace regulated by predictable shifts on duty. Time is understood as an absolute but drawing on anthropological explorations of time and work, this chapter explores how a flexible ontology of time opens space to reconsider our means of establishing urgency (through imperfect 'tools for reckoning time' (Birth, 2012) and the work that it is possible to do in a moment.

Keywords The clock · Temporality · Ontologies of time

The clock on the kitchen wall ticks loudly, marking the passage of time in regulated tick tick ticks, propelling us into a future that is always unfolding at the same pace. Trying to sleep in an unfamiliar house, the loud ticking disturbs rest. On an average day at home the clock marks the countdown to school drop offs: Have you brushed your teeth? Rush rush, put on your shoes and your coat? Rush rush, we're going to miss the bell! At work the hours of the day are counted and tallied up for our pay. Accumulating 7.5 hours a

© The Author(s) 2020
K. McKinnon, *Birthing Work*,
https://doi.org/10.1007/978-981-15-0010-7_7

day, 38 hours a week, I earn my wages through the contribution of time, my labours valued by the hour.

Deep in labour and working towards the birth of my third child, time no longer passes according to the regulated patter of the clock. I take a marker of the time at 10am when I am on all fours on the floor, breathing my way through the contractions. My two young children get bored of rubbing my back and decide to use me as a climbing frame. Clearly it is time to send them off to a friend's house to play. Once the children have gone, time passes from breath to breath, contraction to contraction. Breathing through the pain, and trying to fully relax in between, making the most of the time to recover before the next one comes. The unfolding time bends to this singular reality. I've passed through the spell of thinking 'Oh god, I remember this now, this is hard, this hurts!' and now I am given over to rhythm of labour, just getting through the next contraction. I've tried lying down, I've leaned against the doorway, sought relief in the shower, and now here it comes, the urge to push – suddenly there's a deadline looming 'Is the pool ready? Why isn't it ready? Get it ready! Why is it taking so long?' Rush rush!! And then the pushing, like being hit by a train, only the train is inside my body and splitting me open.

In the distance, I can hear the whistle of the steam engine. It's the 11.45 Castlemaine-Maldon steam train. I get in the pool at last. I push again, and again the whistle blows. I am still pushing, and it is taking an eternity. My breath catches at the top of my throat and she crowns. Another whistle – is this train never leaving? At last another contraction and another push and her head is out. I cradle her head in my hand and wait now for the next one. Waiting waiting, still that damned train hasn't left the station, I can hear the whistle blow. But at last the final contraction comes and she slips out into my arms and I bring her up gently through the water and hold her to me. It has taken forever.

It is now 11.47.

The clock makes us think time unfolds with unending and unwavering regularity, tick tick tick. The clock seems to hold a universal truth: that time is the same always and everywhere, that its counting of the minutes and hours as they pass is just how the world is, nothing more nothing less. But the marking of time in such a way is not neutral. As in all areas of life, the cadence of time as we experience it varies. It speeds up and slows down.

As with all others who are present in the birthing room, the clock brings its own particular expectations and creates its own possibilities. When the clock is put to work to mark the passage of time, it *does* something in that birthing room—it brings into being a birth very different from one timed breath-to-breath, contraction-to-contraction. Time has become a concern well before labour begins: as the weeks of pregnancy pass, and a baby becomes 'overdue' after the 40-week mark (or the 40th, 41st or 43rd week depending on which source one consults). But it is during labour in hospital, and at home, that the clock is really put to work to measure how well a woman is progressing. When the clock is put to work, it is the (regulated and linear) passing of time itself that becomes important. In this chapter I show how the presence of the clock shifts what we attend to during labour. Listening for the ticking of passing seconds makes it harder to focus on the different ways labour may change as time goes on, the different ways a mother may reach exhaustion, or the different ways a child may become distressed.

TIME IS NOT EVERYTHING

Time is often understood as a universal fact of life, but human relationships with time have changed drastically as we have learned to measure and mark it in different ways. The clock has become a ubiquitous presence in our global society over the last 300 years, accompanying the spread of industrialisation and its transformation of the workplace. While the passing of time has always been measured, before the clock, the means of doing so was embedded in the cultural rhythms of place and practice, and the rhythms of the sun through the sky: 'In Madagascar time might be measured by a "rice-cooking" (about half an hour) or "the frying of a locust" (a moment)' (Thompson, 1967, p. 58). Among the Nandi, according to Thompson, the progression of the day proceeded in half-hour units: 'at 6 the sheep have been unfastened, at 6.30 the sun has grown, at 7 it has become warm' (1967, p. 58). Measurements were tied to the tasks of daily life, the rising of the sun, and the sense that things take as long as they take (not that a task should be crammed into a timed section of the day). Pierre Bourdieu observed in Algeria 'an attitude of submission and of nonchalant indifference to the passage of time which no-one dreams of mastering, using up or saving... Haste is seen as a lack of decorum combined with diabolical ambition' (cited in Thompson, 1967, pp. 58–59).

Anthropologist Kevin Birth (2012) offers a compelling picture of how different modes of time-keeping reveal a temporal complexity; rich and varied ways of reckoning time that were specific to places, cultures and seasons. He argues that the global adoption of clock-time has meant a worldwide loss of this complexity. Birth points out that the standardised authority of clock-time has not grown from natural earthly and celestial rhythms: standardised time is the subject of bureaucratic decision-making. It is the recommendations of a committee (the International Telecommunication Union's Radiocommunication Sector, or ITU-R, Working Part 7A) which keep the atomic clocks of the Bureau International des Poids et Mesures (BPIM) in sync with the wobbles of the Earth's rotation (and are in turn, Birth argues, closely tied to relations of power and the rise of capitalism).

The emergence of a uniform accounting of time has had significant impacts on how we work. Thompson's analysis of archival evidence in the UK indicates that the clock introduced a new way of measuring the progression of the day and a new way of valuing labour. Thompson argues that before labour was 'timed by the clock', work tended to be oriented to the task at hand and unfold alongside and simultaneous to life. But now an 'employer must *use* the time of his labour, and see it is not wasted: not the task but the value of time when reduced to money is dominant. Time is now currency: it is not passed but spent' (p. 61). The clock itself mediated the emergence of new relationships with time and new labour relations.

This same shift of work rhythm applies to health care. For a doctor in the nineteenth century attending the sick was a task undertaken as needed, at the patient's home. As medical care became institutionalised, it became more common for those in need to travel to see the doctor, rather than the other way around. And it became common that they did so only during 'office hours' (Davis-Floyd, 2003; Kedgley, 1996). The unpredictability of birth, and the fact that women often go into labour at unsociable hours of the night, is a reason given for many doctors abandoning the practice of attending births. It is hard to be permanently available for the women you are caring for: One of our interviewees, Michael, was also one of the last working GP Obstetricians in New Zealand and spoke of the fact that *'there's getting up at night. There's not having any privacy in your life … that was part of my life for 40 years'*.

Although hospitals are open 24 hours a day, the midwives and obstetricians attending a birth are still working to the clock—they have a shift time that begins and ends.[1] Time has become money in a hospital setting as well, and there is an accompanying pressure to time births to fit within the working day: intervening to speed up labour or recommending a caesarean

---

[1] Trudy Stevens (2010) makes the point that contemporary caseload midwifery has in effect reintroduced a pre-industrial time frame for work, with midwives work patterns following the needs of women and the unpredictable timing of labour.

section in order to avoid an interrupted weekend. The classic example is of the obstetrician that gets a woman to agree to a scheduled caesarean so that they won't miss their Saturday morning game of golf, but there are real financial costs as well. As Michael pointed out:

> *If I am bringing the theatre in at 11 o'clock at night, that is costing a lot of money for you and me as taxpayers. If you were to choose to have an elective caesar at nine o'clock on a Monday morning, you're on a routine list. All the staff are being paid anyway. It was just the cost of the gas, or the poisons that they stick into you for your spinal anaesthetic. So, it's not like it's a huge expense.*

The costs of a caesarean section, a procedure that the World Health Organization recommends should only be conducted for medically indicated reasons (necessary in only 10–15% pregnancies on average, World Health Organization, 2015), are dramatically reduced if the operation is scheduled rather than conducted as a response to emerging problems during childbirth. Financial imperatives and health imperatives do not blend well in this case. The clock makes it much more appealing, financially, to book a caesarean in rather than wait until it is absolutely necessary.

The Clock Tracks 'Progress'

The work of labour takes time. The presence of the clock creates a birth that is ruled by a regulated passing of time, a counting of time, rather than a generous sense of a process unfolding. There is a clock in most hospital birthing rooms, usually set high on the wall, in a central position in the room. While time-keeping is supposed to help carers be attentive to risk, and to map individual women against an average curve of progress, in fact, what my stories point to is that often the clock is instead allowed to *direct* labour. In obstetric and midwifery manuals, in the guidelines enshrined in hospital policy, the time-keeping role of the clock figures highly. As childbirth educator, Susan Ross said to me: *Once you're in a hospital there is the pressure of the clock.*

The practice of obstetric attentiveness to time was well established before women began to routinely give birth in hospitals. Guidelines based on 'prevailing observations about average labour duration and outcomes' informed such advice as 'never let the sun set twice on a labouring woman' (Cohen & Friedman, 2015, p. 420). But the advent of the clock, and new temporalities of the industrial age, brought enormous changes to how the timing of labour was managed (McCourt & Dykes, 2010). Key to contemporary forms of time-based control rest on the work of Emanuel Friedman whose observations of more than 500 births created a new evidence base around the normal parameters of dilation and descent, measured as a function of centimetres dilated to hours of active labour. The resulting 'Friedman's curve' remains in use today as a guide to the average duration of labour and the foundation for hospital policies as to when labour may be lasting 'too long' and begins to become a 'risk factor'. An internal examination assesses dilation of the cervix, and this is set against the number of hours counted as 'active labour', to create a measure of progress. The guidelines for how many hours a women ought to labour are ideally placed alongside the accepted knowledge that every birth is different. The World Health Organization (2018) emphasises that the standard duration of labour can vary widely for each woman, but in practice averages are used to set thresholds of risk beyond which women are not permitted to stray. Within a certain number of hours of active labour commencing, the birthing woman ought to have dilated so many centimetres. From the perspective of the clock, when a birth starts to deviate from this set of parameters, things can get risky, and hospitals therefore attend to it closely. The consequences of failing to perform to the clock can be significant (as Laura's story in Chapter 5 demonstrates) both in terms of the possible outcomes that more time in labour can signify, and in the way medical systems respond to the passing of time. Labouring is hard work for both mother and child, and as time passes, one or both may get worn out, muscles may stop working as they should, and foetal heart rates can become elevated signalling distress.

In a modern maternity care setting, being aware of the risks of passing time and responding quickly to prevent injury or death, is of paramount concern. As New Zealand midwife, Jane, noted, in-hospital professionals working under a 'medical model' and working with 'time factors in their head' are waiting for things to go wrong:

> *If we don't watch it closely, it's just death, disaster, destruction and they sit there waiting with that perspective in their head… They have got time factors in their head and it must be going according to plan. Whereas midwifery is much more, just let it happen, give it time. We can't put it in a box. Let it do its own thing.*
> *So you've got these two totally - fighting over and fighting over the space because that is coming into that space. So if say for example labour is not progressing particularly well for someone, a midwifery approach might be okay, let*

*her have a rest for a little bit. It's okay that she hasn't progressed her one cen-
timetre in the hour. Take that CTG off, get her in the bath, give her a massage,
let her chill down for a bit. Things like lighting and music, all that sort of stuff,
you will think about it much more holistically and try and tune in a bit more.
Whereas medically they would be, well, Crack the [Syntocinon] and crack on.
She is not performing and that's it.*

What Jane is describing is an attitude that leads to what is known as a 'cascade of intervention' (discussed in Chapter 1). If progress is slow, a gentle
approach might be to get a woman to try moving, changing her position,
or altering her environment. In a hospital setting a common intervention,
however, is the use of a synthetic hormone, such as Syntocinon, to intensify the contractions and speed the process. Under Syntocinon, the pain of
contractions often intensifies, so many women turn to an epidural for pain
relief. This in turn slows labour down again. As labour slows, a mother is
more likely to be diagnosed with 'failure to progress', meaning things are
moving at a rate slower than the average.

A 2013 study found that more than 1 in 3 (35%) of the Caesareans given
to first-time mothers were due to a diagnosis of 'failure to progress', or slow
progress in labour (Boyle et al., 2013). The evidence suggests that many of
them were still in very early labour when they were told that they were not
dilating fast enough, meaning they were likely to have been given even less
time than the averages suggest is normal. According to the literature, good
obstetrics practice ideally attends less to the clock and more to signs of
progress and indications of whether or not a slow labour may spell trouble.
Friedman's curve was never intended to be used as a regulatory device
(Cohen & Friedman, 2015) and more recent studies have shown that rates
of dilation often are much slower today than in the 1950s, when Friedman
conducted his study (Dekker, 2017), especially if modern anaesthetics are
being used.

The anxiety that something might go wrong stems from the knowledge
that a stalled labour can indeed be life-threatening. Rebecca, a New Zealand
mother, told us the story of how the option of an emergency caesarean
section really did save her life and the life of her child. In the labour of
her first child, her circumstances fall under a classic pattern of 'failure to
progress'. Her waters had broken but labour was not kicking in, so she was
given Syntocinon to get things moving. The labour pains were very strong
(as is often the case with an induction) so she then was given an epidural,
and 40 hours after her waters broke was advised that she should have a

caesarean, because '*You are dilating but we don't know if we'd have any luck with getting the baby out that way. If we have a caesarean now, we know the baby's still okay and blah, blah... So it was over to us*'. Rebecca followed the advice she was given because '*We thought they actually did know what they were talking about. So we were quite happy for that to go ahead*'. The decision was made calmly, and it was in no way an emergency. However, 18 months later with her second pregnancy, things were different:

Jet's was the most traumatic because we'd planned to do the ... vaginal birth after caesarean [VBAC] and thought that should have been absolutely fine. We were told there was a one or two per cent chance there can be some dehiscence, which is when the old scars open up basically. I was feeling really good, I had great pregnancies and was feeling very positive about the whole birthing experience.

Because of the caesarean 18 months before, they were monitoring, so I did have to have some devices attached to me ... I just remember doing the same stuff, needing to kneel down and lean on the bed or something to try and get through contractions. ... we were in there for a couple of hours but it showed up that Jet was in distress, I think her heart rate accelerated really fast or something like that. So they then said, Okay we need, we are going to need to go and probably do another caesarean on this one ... they couldn't tell exactly but they knew something was wrong internally with me probably, for the baby to be having all that distress.

So, we need to... do a caesarean, an emergency C-section. It's not elective in any way. So alright, that was more freaky... I was in there with my midwife and I was still having these huge contractions and they were just really, really full on. In between things, in the separate world, I'm in my own head mainly but I'm aware of little bits going on. I remember them saying to the anaesthetist, okay we're just monitoring, we need to move really quickly on this one. I'm like, just do whatever you have to do, you know, just get the baby out. I was really freaking... it was really obvious because I had a very lovely calm midwife who suddenly was very calm but very firm that we needed to be faster. It was like, shit, my baby, because we hadn't thought that we'd go down that sort of track. ... So yes, they gave me a general anaesthetic so I was out for that and didn't know anything until I woke up in the recovery room, which is kind of a weird – again, you're in the basement of a hospital, no light... Then the midwife had written on my hand, it's a girl, which was really helpful. [Laughs] ... it was really good that they'd done it but it was really freaky at the time, just knowing at the moment before going into surgery, realising at that point that, shit, this is really serious, this could go badly wrong.

What had gone wrong was that her uterus had begun to rupture as the layers of stitching from the first caesarean began to open up. Without the emergency procedure both she and Jet would have been in trouble. When she consulted the surgeon the next day, he informed her that there had been a lot of scar tissue from the previous caesarean, '*which is why I always think, why would women ever opt to have a caesarean if … there wasn't a medical reason for doing so? Because it messes things up*'. While the consequences of 'failure to progress' can be dire, so too can the consequences of administering a caesarean, including implications for future pregnancies as well as all the risks that go along with major abdominal surgery.

Along with other actors in the birthing space, the clock has a role to play in making it more difficult for labour to progress. This is especially so when the clock insists that we pay attention to it and that birthing women perform to it. Meg relates how it felt when she arrived at hospital after her labour began:

> *When I got to the hospital, I felt that I was under a little bit more pressure to perform. Because now I'm here and everybody's looking at you and if you don't reach this certain milestone by eight o'clock tonight then we're going to have to do something else.*

The uncompromising attitude of the ticking clock, and those who use it to pressure women to perform, denies a birth its own periodicity; it is giving over instead to the parameters set by time. It does not make the birthing space one that is conducive to the feeling of being in 'the zone', in a space that is dark or quiet or loving. As midwife Jane remarked,

> *We are expecting women to perform a deeply, emotional, personal experience in a really stark, dire environment that's not really conducive to letting go. They have only been there a short while and they are expected to feel safe and comfortable because you need to feel safe. So it's quite an ask, I think, what we are asking women to do in that environment.*

The clock's pressure to perform can counteract a woman's effort to successfully establish labour. Rather than encouraging the contractions to intensify or speed up, the stress of performance seems most likely to slow things down. Recall Laura, whose story was introduced in Chapter 5. Working towards a VBAC (Vaginal Birth After Caesarean) under the care of a female obstetrician, she was given a clear message that failure to perform to the clock would result in a caesarean section: *Even though I was trying to be active and up and about, I was also just in this panic mode of, Crap that hurts, crap they're going to come and get me any minute now—like my frame of mind wasn't in the right place, it wasn't how I should be feeling.* The panic that 'any minute now' they would come and get her, the fear that her body would not progress, never really left Laura's birthing room. And in the end, it was the clock, and the assessment that she had 'failed to progress', that determined her delivery by caesarean section.

MANAGING TIME

While the clock is ubiquitous, it is also a presence in the birthing room that many midwives work with consciously, often by taking it down, or covering it up, or positioning the woman in labour so that she cannot see it. Helen, a Sydney mum who birthed in hospital, remembers '*a big clock above the bed, because at one stage when I was in labour, I was on the ball, looking up at the clock and every time I looked up at it the clock would barely be moving*'. Her midwife noticed that she was looking at the clock and intervened '[She] *said, no, let's rearrange you. So she moved me somewhere else and had me standing up and holding on to [my husband] and then I think time went a bit quicker*'. For a woman coping with the pain of labour and struggling to work towards the time when labour will be over and a baby will be born, the clock acts to slow down what is unfolding. The labouring is hard work and the counting of time engenders a desire for time to speed up, for the labour to move faster so that it is possible to reach the end of it more quickly. Teresa, who birthed at a different hospital in Sydney, found herself watching the clock on the wall above: '*I'm just watching the clock the whole time. There's a clock - worst idea ever*'. Going into transition, commonly the moment when labour can be most intense, she remembered, '*I'm just watching the clock the whole time - hurry up*'. Her attendants said, '*Oh, it will go quicker if your waters break. I'm like, break my waters then!*'

By contrast, when the clock is covered up or removed from view, time is permitted to unfold differently, and the progress of labour becomes marked not by the agonising slow movement of the minute hand but breath by breath, contraction by contraction. Women still speak of waiting for it to end, and of counting the number of contractions to measure their way through the labour. But the counting of contractions marks time in a different way—each one is a step towards the birth of a child, each contraction a woman gets through is one less contraction she will have to endure before she holds a baby in her arms. Many midwives in this study spoke about how much easier it can be when a woman feels that the road before her is getting shorter bit by bit, and that the pain has purpose. This knowledge turns time to a woman's advantage, helping her to get through the experience.

Take the story of Laura's third birth for example. Laura's third child was birthed under a very different care regime from her first two. Unwilling to return again to the care of her obstetrician or the hospital that she felt had bullied her into two consecutive caesareans, she discovered that it was possible to have a homebirth. With the support of an independent midwife and a doula, this time she was allowed to labour slowly at home. The first contractions began on a Monday afternoon, and through a night and a day of getting in and out of the bath, going into the garden, taking rests, cooking pasta, and opening presents for her son's birthday, she finally got into the birth pool at about 8 p.m. on the Tuesday night. When her midwife arrive at 8:30,

> *I was so comfortable that I didn't even really acknowledge her. I was just, I don't know, I was just really relaxed and really just into what was happening and not worrying about it and just – we were sitting in this practically pitch black room and everyone's just in silence.*

When her waters finally broke and she started to push there was no external pressure to do anything, other than the instruction from her midwife to 'follow her body':

> *I didn't really have control over what was happening then. It was like my body decided to push – my brain wasn't a part of it. It was funny, because she kept saying things to me like, you know, Do you want to feel for your baby's head, do you want to have a look. I couldn't even answer her, because I was just in the zone. They even had little quiet conversations around me – I just wasn't a part of it, I wasn't aware of it... I just can't believe how relaxed I was. The whole thing. I'd have my moments of, what about this, okay, and then I'd just go back into it. I was just so comfortable. It was painful as all hell. This is what I said to my husband later – it's not that it didn't hurt, it was painful as all hell, but it was, I don't know, it was, that was how it was supposed to be. It was a good pain; it was worth it.*

For Laura, the sense of strength and achievement that came from this was enormous:

> *.. her head came out first and then her whole body came out and the midwife*
> *said to me, sit back and pick up your baby... This moment would have been two*
> *seconds, but felt like 10 minutes .... I just scooped her up and I was just like, oh*
> *my gosh, like I'm the first person to hold my baby. I'm the first person she's looking*
> *at. Like this was just – for me. It wasn't even, I didn't even cry, because I was*
> *just kind of so in awe of the whole thing – that it had happened and I'd done it*
> *and that I didn't need 20 people standing around me to do it, you know.*

It was a birth that followed the body rather than the clock, and the results for Laura were awe-inspiring.

The work to help a birthing mother see (and feel) time differently was something that Sarah, a midwife in New Zealand, also recognised as important. She identified as her '*proudest midwifery moment*' in achieving this for a woman whose first two experiences had been traumatic. While supporting this woman through her third birth in a New Zealand hospital, Sarah says she worked hard to make it 'beautiful':

> *I had a client having her third baby, and she hadn't had her first two with me.*
> *She was terrified of birth. She'd had a forceps and a ventouse. Birth was just*
> *a horrendous event for her... So, for that family, they wanted the child, [but]*
> *they didn't want the birth. I worked so hard around all of those issues in trying*
> *to make her trust me, because even if she didn't trust herself, if she trusted me*
> *that everything was okay, then maybe that would be all right... I remember her*
> *getting to transition and being like, 'I can't', as women do. I can't, I need an*
> *epidural. I said to her, you are nearly there. If you can do 10 more contractions,*
> *I will check, and if you're not fully dilated, I will get you an epidural.*
>
> *Her partner was looking at me, because they were really hanging on me*
> *holding it together for them. I looked at him and I gave him a big smile and*
> *we counted her through those 10 contractions and at the end of it, she was fully*
> *dilated and had a beautiful water birth ... She wrote me this beautiful card*
> *afterwards, saying thank you for showing me that birth isn't a horrible, horrible*
> *thing.*

Even when the outcome is not what the mother had wanted, giving a sense of spaciousness, holding back the pressure of time, seemed to make a difference for many women. Remember Meg (whose story is told in Chapter 2). Her unexpected caesarean still felt empowering, and this is partly down to how her carers negotiated with time. When she was asked if there was anything she would have done differently, she said:

No, because we did everything. It was a long time, we had the time to do every-thing. I was given the option to do everything and this is why I don't have any hang ups about my c-section. Because I don't go back saying, I wonder if I'd done that, maybe this would have been the outcome. Because there was no outcome going that way because we'd tried that path, we did it already.

CONCLUSION: MAKING TIME WORK

To work with birth, and the accompanying technologies and bureaucracies and doctors and midwives and mothers and families and bodies and babies, takes time. Our interviews highlighted the pressures of time in the birth space and how the clock often regulated and policed women's labours. The clock constitutes a birth that proceeds according to the regulated mechanism of the steady count of seconds and minutes. Rather than allowing the labouring woman and her carers to 'attend upon what is an observed necessity' the clock introduces the urgency of 'timed labour' (Thompson, 1967, p. 60). Time marked by the clock becomes currency, a mode we are all familiar with through the adage 'time is money'. And when it is time that is the focus, rather than the task we are engaged in, the time a woman spends in labour becomes important—more important, somehow, than the innate rhythm of the task. It is the tick tick tick that is attended to, rather than timing given breath-to-breath, contraction-to-contraction. While it is meant to impose precision and regularity to our perceptions of time, in birth, the clock has the strange effect of warping time. Time seems to slow down: a mere five minutes in transition, as the baby pushes past the cervix and into the birth passage, slows down and seems to last forever. But more than this, the presence of the clock can in fact slow down labour. The pressure to perform, to be given a deadline, introduces such stress that labour can grind to a halt.

Some women have babies quickly, others have labours that last for days. How does a carer balance the particularities of any given woman's labour against guidelines that set the clock as the prominent arbiter of whether a labour is going well or not? The stories recounted here suggest that it is the clock and its relentless marking of time that comes to the fore in the hospital labouring room, where the calibrated measurement of time has an affinity with an institution dominated by technologies of measurement, and a workplace regulated by predictable shifts on duty. The clock measures the minutes and seconds that may pass as carers wait to intervene and save a life. Responding to the clock, the anxiety that passing time produces feeds into what actions carers may take or recommend. Birth by the clock is valued by the hour and labour unfolds through each passing minute—a very different thing to the cadence and timing of the body's contractions.

The clock does not have to rule the birthing space, although it is often allowed to. It may be moved, covered, overruled. Its measurements of individual labours may be placed alongside a spectrum of possibility, rather than being used to police an average. Time might seem a neutral and universal thing, but in fact it wavers, it bends, it follows different cadences not all of which adhere to the mechanics of a clock. Time may be made to work with a labouring mother, rather than against her.

References

Birth, K. K. (2012). *Objects of time*. https://doi.org/10.1057/9781137017895.

Boyle, A., Reddy, U. M., Landy, H. J., Huang, C.-C., Driggers, R. W., & Laughon, S. K. (2013). Primary cesarean delivery in the United States. *Obstetrics and Gynecology, 122*(1), 33–40. https://doi.org/10.1097/AOG.0b013e3182952242.

Cohen, W. R., & Friedman, E. A. (2015). Perils of the new labor management guidelines. *American Journal of Obstetrics and Gynecology, 212*(4), 420–427. https://doi.org/10.1016/j.ajog.2014.09.008.

Davis-Floyd, R. (2003). *Birth as an American rite of passage*. Berkeley: University of California Press.

Dekker, R. (2017, April 26). Friedman's curve and failure to progress: A leading cause of unplanned cesareans. *Evidence Based Birth*. https://evidencebasedbirth.com/friedmans-curve-and-failure-to-progress-a-leading-cause-of-unplanned-c-sections/.

Kedgley, S. J. (1996). *Mum's the word: The untold story of motherhood in New Zealand*. Auckland: Random House New Zealand.

McCourt, C., & Dykes, F. (2010). From tradition to modernity: Time and childbirth in historial perspective. *Childbirth, midwifery and concepts of time* (pp. 17–36). Oxford: Berghann Books.

Stevens, T. (2010). Time and Midwifery Practice. In C. McCourts (Ed.), *Childbirth, midwifery and concepts of time* (pp. 104–125). New York: Berghahn Books.

Thompson, E. P. (1967). Time, work-discipline, and industrial capitalism. *The Past and Present Society, 38*, 56–97.

World Health Organization. (2015). *WHO | WHO statement on caesarean section rates*. http://www.who.int/reproductivehealth/publications/maternal_perinatal_health/cs-statement/en/.

World Health Organization. (2018). *WHO recommendation on duration of the first stage of labour.* https://extranet.who.int/rhl/topics/preconception-pregnancy-childbirth-and-postpartum-care/care-during-childbirth/care-during-labour-1st-stage/who-recommendation-duration-first-stage-labour.

CHAPTER 8

Conclusion: Caring for the Diverse Birth

Abstract This chapter pulls together the threads of the childbirth assemblage. I suggest that in place of the wars over which care model is 'right', a better approach is to *think with* this knowledge of the multiplicity of birth. Given that there is an ontological plurality in the birthing space, I argue that the childbirth assemblage described in this book could be understood as a collective, and the work of childbirth as the shared responsibility of that collective. The frequent references to 'teamwork' by the midwives and obstetricians in the study signal an opening for this understanding. In the concluding section, I propose eight companions accompany us in the work of childbirth. They are part of the 'team' who conduct this collective work, whose contributions and allegiances can be gathered to the support of a positive—even empowering—experience of birth.

Keywords Ontology · Multiple ontologies · Weak theory · Birthing collectives · Maternal work

The challenges of mothering, and the maternal anxieties that go with it, are a favourite topic of conversation among most mothers in my community. Our negotiations around how to care for our children well, while making a living, while nurturing our relationships, while fulfilling our obligations, while finding joy and love and connection, touch everything from

© The Author(s) 2020   123
K. McKinnon, *Birthing Work*,
https://doi.org/10.1007/978-981-15-0010-7_8

the briefest exchanges in the schoolyard to the deep and meaningful conversations we snatch over a cup of tea. A shadow over many of these exchanges is the mother-blame and mother-guilt that many of us are forced to contend with, hidden in the casual question of 'Who is looking after your kids today?'—asked often of mothers in the workplace, but never of fathers. While parents of all kinds discuss and negotiate the challenges of nurturing and caring for children, there are some particular challenges that seem to only apply to women. Another shadow is in the suggestion that we have got it all wrong: whether it is that we failed to breastfeed, or we breastfed too much and in the wrong places; that we put our child's microbiome at risk for choosing a caesarean section, or we put their lives at risk by choosing a homebirth; that we are neglecting them by putting them into childcare, or we are failing to live up to our potential by staying at home to care for them. There are many wonderful writers who are seeking to disrupt this litany of maternal inadequacies, and one of these is Chris Bobel. Bobel is concerned about the damage that mother-blame narratives can do. She reminds us that:

> *Mothering does make a difference and sometimes that difference is negative.* But to place the complex individual and social problems squarely on the backs of mothers amounts to sexist and counterproductive scapegoating. Further, this distortion siphons attention from finding solutions that benefit our children by supporting mothers. We are *collectively* responsible for how our children turn out, because the care of children takes place in a social context. (Bobel, 2004, p. 76 emphasis original)

In this book I have argued that accepting this collective responsibility ought to begin through pregnancy and childbirth by rethinking maternal work as a collective endeavour.

Childbirth is influenced by a vast array of contributing factors, and the different roles played by all actors, human and non-human, affect how the experience unfolds. One consequence of this understanding should be a sense of disquiet with narratives that suggest that decisions made by birthing mothers alone, or by carers alone, are what determine birth outcomes in an absolute sense. This book suggests that, on the contrary, what happens during a birth is the result, not just of what people do, but of what *things* do. It is not just people that are present and shape childbirth, but the things that surround and support us (from technologies and institutions, to the furniture in the birth space); the biophysical processes and chemical flows within the body (including the hormones that regulate labour and blood that transports oxygen and chemical signals to the baby); and the natural world within which we dwell (providing water that comforts during labour or the sunshine that many women avoid). When a child is born, a great many different things, and people, and ideas and beliefs and objects and technologies gather around and help to shape that birth—no single one of them is solely in charge. In this book part of my task has been to unravel who and what some of these assembled actors are, to understand what it is that these things do, and what the relationships are between them. What this also implies is that all of these things are responsible; that the actors that assemble in childbirth have a *collective* effect on what unfolds, and ought then, to take responsibility as a collective.

I have also sought to elaborate how what these myriad actors do is *work*. The kind of work they do is effortful, conscious, and productive, and it forms the first relations of dependency from which a child will emerge. Babies and bodies must work together, communicating from early pregnancy through bodily signals of tiredness, nausea, through kicking feet and prodding elbows, through chemical messages in the blood. Midwives and doctors must work with a woman's body, listening to it through testing and touching, and speaking back, whether through medical interventions or simply through the quietness of a room. Institutions are at work too, policies and rules and regulations, always watchful over the shoulders of carers. Things and technologies shape what is possible, with the history and intention of their manufacture calling us to respond unquestioningly—and so we lie on the bed, we use the machine. All of this work is conscious and intentional, in different ways. The objects themselves may not be conscious but they carry the conscious intention with which they were made. Likewise, a woman in the 'zone', far away from reasoned thought or careful speech, may not easily be called to self-possession, but she is working from a different kind of consciousness particular to the shared body-mind work of labour. All these different kinds of work, undertaken by different kinds of actors, who are recognised differently (or not at all), and compensated differently (with payment, or gratitude, or love, or care, or sometimes with nothing at all), accumulate to the shared endeavour of maternal work.

What this maternal work produces depends a lot on how the different actors work collectively. Unless tragedy strikes a baby will be born, and woman will become a mother. But whether a mother emerges from the experience empty and frightened, or awestruck and in love, or something in between, has a lot to do with who has been gathered in her childbirth assemblage, and how they have worked together.

The recognition and appreciation of the work done by multiple actors in childbirth also has ontological implications. Ontology, put simply, is a word for how we understand reality. When we speak about ontologies in the plural, we are suggesting that there are different understandings of reality. This is different from saying that we all have different perspectives on the same reality, that we might all see it differently but in essence the true and concrete world is out there and unchanging, regardless of what we think about it. The recognition of multiple ontologies suggests that instead, reality actually is, concretely and materially, different for different people (Law, 2004; Mol & Law, 2004).

As the stories throughout this book have shown, with so many active elements attending and involved in childbirth, there is seldom any singularity to the birth experience. By applying the idea of multiple ontologies it becomes possible to see that perhaps childbirth is not only experienced differently by different people, not only does it feel different, it really *is* different. Even within the same room different actors are attending and becoming involved in entirely different births. The mothers, the midwives, the obstetricians, are not just witnessing and experiencing the same event differently but in fact attending materially different events.

One of the implications of accepting ontological difference in childbirth is to accept that there is no one way to conduct birthing work. The combined colloquial wisdom of mothers and their caregivers shared in this book illuminate the diverse experiences of childbirth. Seeking an understanding of birth through these stories, I have sought to respect the fact that each person is telling their own truths, and by way of historical research have sought to also uncover what stories the voiceless objects in the room can tell. The lessons that may be distilled from these stories can only remain true to the diversity of these wisdoms by maintaining an anti-essentialist stance, in other words, a stance that refuses that any singular universal truth might be located among these varied views and experiences.

Instead, what I offer is what Eve Sedgwick might call a 'weak theory' of birthing work (Sedgwick, 2002). Sedgwick posits weak theory as a feminist counterpoint to 'strong theory', in which the theorist is able to claim authoritative (paranoid) knowledge about what is what, where answers are concrete and clear; these are theories that claim to be able to tell us what is *really* going on in the world. In strong theory there is no room for uncertainty, no room for the recognition that our knowledge, *all* knowledge, is incomplete, or that Others might legitimately know differently. A feminist approach, Sedgwick teaches us, does not need to be so defensive. Thus 'weak theory' can offer understandings of what is really going on in the world, while remaining open to the possibility of different knowledges, different practices, being both possible and legitimate.

My weak theory of birthing work is constituted in lessons distilled from the stories and conversations and explorations of childbirth shared with participants, colleagues, and co-thinkers in the course of this research. From the threads of the childbirth assemblage that I have described throughout this book I want to highlight eight companions in the birth space. In my list below, numbers 1–7 correspond to the themes explored in each chapter of this book, but the eighth—love—is instead a theme that runs across all of them and is an abiding concern in the practice of maternal work. As James, Sydney obstetrician and researcher, remarked in Chapter 5, a '*prime need for labouring women is the need to be loved*'. The imperative for love, as midwife Jane remarked, is not just '*hippy crystals*'. To birth well a woman needs copious flows of oxytocin in her bloodstream, and oxytocin is also the hormone of love, the chemical of mother–baby attachment and thus the foundation of human relationships.

These eight companions accompany us in the work of childbirth. They are part of the 'team' who conduct this collective work, whose contributions and allegiances can be gathered to the support of a positive—even empowering—experience of birth:

1. The assemblage itself: the way childbirth unfolds is the combined effect of a myriad of actors entangled in the space of birth. The assembled parts are never exactly the same, what each actor does or how it interacts with another, can be managed but never controlled. The variables shift, each actor does its own thing, and has effects that may or may not be predicted. The assemblage is not a machine, its parts fitting together to make a purposeful whole. Each part is its own actor, whose role must be attended to, cared for, tinkered with, *midwifed*, along the way.

2. A baby: whatever the tangled legalities of when a baby is meant to come into its own personhood, one thing that was clear from our interviews was that women were forming relationships with their children from the beginning. Even in the midst of childbirth a baby will do its own thing, perhaps pushing herself out, perhaps refusing to

move. A live baby is not just an outcome of birth but an active participant.

3. A body: and not just any body, but an individual woman's body and an intelligent body. A body that may work or may go on strike. A body that may birth beautifully no matter the environment, or a body that may need careful coaxing, gentle touch, subtle communication. A fearful body, or a body that feels safe. Bodies that respond and bodies that resist. Childbirth is an experience that is intensely embodied and there are many different kinds of bodies in the world.

4. Things: the inert stuff in the room is never just stuff, but stuff can be moved, spaces reshaped, and beds wheeled into the corridor.

5. Institutions, laws, policies, regulations: are unavoidable and often obsessed with fixed parameters, pigeonholing, and strict hierarchies. But institutions are also made up of intelligent, creative, and empathetic human beings.

6. Technologies: can save lives, but can also make labour more difficult. They can inform and reassure at the same time as they prompt unnecessary anxieties and undermine embodied knowledge. There is no reason why the body and the machine cannot be comfortable allies.

7. Time: which can always be on our side, especially if the anxieties of the ticking clock can be held at bay, and a space held open for labour to unfold safely in its own time.

8. Love: is not always the dominant emotion in the birth space, although it could and should be. Oxytocin is crucial to labour, and it is also the chemical imprint of love and feelings of safety, trust, empathy and connection. If life begins in birth, so too do our human relationships. Seek to begin these in love ought to be simple common sense.

These companions are present at many, if not all, births. Like companions in life, they do not always work peacefully together. But even when troubled, or unruly, or silent, these companions are doing work in the birth space; effortful, often conscious, always interdependent, work. Gathering them productively into a collective endeavour of childbirth seems a sensible thing to do, and to thereby acknowledge both our collective stake in the outcomes of childbirth, and our collective responsibility in conducting the maternal work that is required.

References

Bobel, C. (2004). When good enough isn't: Mother blame in the continuum concept. *Journal of the Association for Research on Mothering, 6*(2), 68–78.

Law, J. (2004). *After method: Mess in social research.* London and New York: Routledge.

Mol, A., & Law, J. (2004). Embodied action, enacted bodies: The example of hypoglycaemia. *Body & Society, 10*(2–3), 43–62. https://doi.org/10.1177/1357034X04042932.

Sedgwick, E. K. (2002). *Touching feeling: Affect, pedagogy, performativity.* Durham, NC: Duke University Press.

BIBLIOGRAPHY

AIHW. (2015). *Maternal deaths low in Australia, but indigenous women remain at greater risk*. Retrieved June 5, 2017, from Australian Institute of Health and Welfare Media Releases website: http://www.aihw.gov.au/media-release-detail/?id=60129551418.

AIHW. (2018). *Maternal deaths in Australia 2016*. Retrieved from Australian Institute of Health and Welfare website: https://www.aihw.gov.au/reports/mothers-babies/maternal-deaths-in-australia-2016/contents/report.

Badruddoja, R., & Motapanyane, M. (Eds.). (2016). *"New maternalisms": Tales of motherwork (dislodging the unthinkable)*. Bradford, ON: Demeter Press.

Banks, A. C. (1999). *Birthchairs, midwives and medicine*. Jackson: University Press of Mississippi.

Baranauckas, C. (2002). Dr. Orvan W. Hess, 96, Dies; Developed fetal heart monitor. *The New York Times*. Retrieved from https://www.nytimes.com/2002/09/16/us/dr-orvan-w-hess-96-dies-developed-fetal-heart-monitor.html.

Barha, C. K., & Galea, L. A. M. (2017). The maternal "baby brain" revisited. *Nature Neuroscience, 20,* 134.

Barker, K. K. (1998). A ship upon a stormy sea: The medicalization of pregnancy. *Social Science & Medicine, 47*(8), 1067–1076. https://doi.org/10.1016/S0277-9536(98)00155-5.

Bennett, J. (2010). *Vibrant matter: A political ecology of things*. Durham and London: Duke University Press.

Birth, K. K. (2012). *Objects of time*. https://doi.org/10.1057/9781137017895.

Bobel, C. (2004). When good enough isn't: Mother blame in the continuum concept. *Journal of the Association for Research on Mothering, 6*(2), 68–78.

Boyer, K. (2018). *Spaces and politics of motherhood*. London: Rowman & Littlefield.

© The Editor(s) (if applicable) and The Author(s), under exclusive license to Springer Nature Singapore Pte Ltd. 2020
K. McKinnon, *Birthing Work*,
https://doi.org/10.1007/978-981-15-0010-7

Boyle, A., Reddy, U. M., Landy, H. J., Huang, C.-C., Driggers, R. W., & Laughon, S. K. (2013). Primary cesarean delivery in the United States. *Obstetrics and Gynecology, 122*(1), 33–40. https://doi.org/10.1097/AOG.0b013e3182952242.

Bryant, L. R. (2014). *Onto-cartography: An ontology of machines and media.* Edinburgh: Edinburgh University Press.

Buckley, S. J. (2005). *Gentle birth, gentle mothering.* Brisbane: One Moon Press.

Buckley, S. J. (2011). Undisturbed birth. *AIMS Journal, 23*(4). Retrieved from https://www.aims.org.uk/journal/item/undisturbed-birth.

Buckley, S. J. (2015). *Hormonal physiology of childbearing: Evidence and implications for women, babies, and maternity care.* Washington, DC: Childbirth Connection Programs, National Partnership for Women & Families.

Charlton, B. G. (2010). The cancer of bureaucracy: How it will destroy science, medicine, education; and eventually everything else. *Medical Hypotheses, 74*(6), 961–965. https://doi.org/10.1016/j.mehy.2009.11.038.

Chatterton, P., & Pickerill, J. (2010). Everyday activism and transitions towards post-capitalist worlds. *Transactions of the Institute of British Geographers, 35*(4), 475–490.

Clark, S. L., & Hankins, G. D. V. (2003). Temporal and demographic trends in cerebral palsy—Fact and fiction. *American Journal of Obstetrics and Gynecology, 188*(3), 628–633. https://doi.org/10.1067/mob.2003.204.

Cohen, W. R., & Friedman, E. A. (2015). Perils of the new labor management guidelines. *American Journal of Obstetrics and Gynecology, 212*(4), 420–427. https://doi.org/10.1016/j.ajog.2014.09.008.

Colls, R., & Fannin, M. (2013). Placental surfaces and the geographies of bodily interiors. *Environment and Planning A, 45,* 1087–1104.

Crabb, A. (2014). *The wife drought.* Sydney, NSW: Ebury Press.

Dahlen, H. (2013, May 7). Stand and deliver—Upright births best for mum and bub. *The Conversation,* p. 4.

Dahlen, H., Downe, S., Kennedy, H. P., & Foureur, M. (2014). Is society being reshaped on a microbiological and epigenetic level by the way women give birth? *Midwifery, 30*(12), 1149–1151. https://doi.org/10.1016/j.midw.2014.07.007.

Dahlen, H., Homer, C. S. E., Cooke, M., Upton, A. M., Nunn, R., & Brodrick, B. (2007). Perineal outcomes and maternal comfort related to the application of perineal warm packs in the second stage of labor: A randomized controlled trial. *Birth, 34*(4), 282–290. https://doi.org/10.1111/j.1523-536X.2007.00186.x.

Dahlen, H., Jackson, M., & Stevens, J. (2011). Homebirth, freebirth and doulas: Casualty and consequences of a broken maternity system. *Women and Birth, 24*(1), 47–50. https://doi.org/10.1016/j.wombi.2010.11.002.

Dahlen, H., Kennedy, H. P., Anderson, C. M., Bell, A. F., Clark, A., Foureur, M., ... Downe, S. (2013). The EPIIC hypothesis: Intrapartum effects on the neonatal epigenome and consequent health outcomes. *Medical Hypotheses, 80*(5), 656–662. https://doi.org/10.1016/j.mehy.2013.01.017.

Davidson, R. J., & Sutton, S. K. (1995). Affective neuroscience: The emergence of a discipline. *Current Opinion in Neurobiology, 5*(2), 217–224. https://doi.org/10.1016/0959-4388(95)80029-8.

Davis, D. L., & Walker, K. (2010). Re-discovering the material body in midwifery through an exploration of theories of embodiment. *Midwifery, 26*(4), 457–462. https://doi.org/10.1016/j.midw.2008.10.004.

Davis-Floyd, R. (1993). The technocratic model of birth. In *Feminist theory in the study of folklore* (pp. 297–326). Urbana and Champaign: University of Illinois Press.

Davis-Floyd, R. (2001). The technocratic, humanistic, and holistic paradigms of childbirth. *International Journal of Gynecology & Obstetrics, 75*, S5–S23. https://doi.org/10.1016/S0020-7292(01)00510-0.

Davis-Floyd, R. (2003). *Birth as an American rite of passage*. Berkeley: University of California Press.

Davis-Floyd, R., & Davis, E. (1996). Intuition as authoritative knowledge in midwifery and homebirth. *Medical Anthropology Quarterly, 10*(2), 237–269. https://doi.org/10.1525/maq.1996.10.2.02a00080.

Davis-Floyd, R., & Sargent, C. (1997). *Childbirth and authoritative knowledge: Cross-cultural perspectives*. Berkeley: University of California Press.

de Beauvoir, S. (1952). *The second sex*. New York: Knopf.

De Lee, J. B. (1920). *The principles and practice of obstetrics*. Philadelphia: WB Saunders Company.

Dekker, R. (2017, April 26). Friedman's curve and failure to progress: A leading cause of unplanned cesareans. *Evidence Based Birth*. Retrieved from https://evidencebasedbirth.com/friedmans-curve-and-failure-to-progress-a-leading-cause-of-unplanned-c-sections/.

Deleuze, G., & Guattari, F. (1987). *A thousand plateaus: Capitalism and schizophrenia*. Minneapolis: University of Minnesota Press.

Dombroski, K. (2018). Learning to be affected: Maternal connection, intuition and "elimination communication." *Emotion, Space and Society, 26*, 72–79. https://doi.org/10.1016/j.emospa.2017.09.004.

Dombroski, K., McKinnon, K., & Healy, S. (2016). Beyond the birth wars: Diverse assemblages of care. *New Zealand Geographer, 72*, 230–239. https://doi.org/10.1111/nzg.12142.

Dundes, L. (1987). The evolution of maternal birthing position. *American Journal of Public Health, 77*(5), 6.

Dunn, P. M. (1999). The Chamberlen family (1560–1728) and obstetric forceps. *Archives of Disease in Childhood—Fetal and Neonatal Edition, 81*(3), F232–F234. https://doi.org/10.1136/fn.81.3.F232.

Eastman, K. S., & Loustaunau, M. O. (1988). Reacting to the medical bureaucracy: Lay midwifery as a birthing alternative. *Marriage & Family Review, 11*(3–4), 23–37. https://doi.org/10.1300/J002v11n03_03.

Escobar, A. (2018). *Designs for the pluriverse.* Durham and London: Duke University Press.

Federici, S. (2012). *Revolution at point zero.* Oakland: PM Press.

Feeley, C., & Thomson, G. (2016). Going it alone. *Midwives, 19*(3), 62–65.

Ferguson, J. (2015). *Give a man a fish: Reflections on the new politics of distribution.* Durham: Duke University Press.

Gao, L., Rabbitt, E., Condon, J., Renthal, N., Johnston, J., & Mitsche, M. (2015). Molecular mechanisms within fetal lungs initiate labor. *Science Daily.* Retrieved from https://www.sciencedaily.com/releases/2015/06/150622162023.htm.

Gao, L., Rabbitt, E. H., Condon, J. C., Renthal, N. E., Johnston, J. M., Mitsche, M. A., … Mendelson, C. R. (2015). Steroid receptor coactivators 1 and 2 mediate fetal-to-maternal signaling that initiates parturition. *The Journal of Clinical Investigation, 125*(7), 2808–2824. https://doi.org/10.1172/JCI78544.

Gaskin, I. M. (2011). *Birth matters: A midwife's manifesta.* New York: Seven Stories Press.

Gibson-Graham, J. K. (2006). *A postcapitalist politics.* Minneapolis: University of Minnesota Press.

Gibson-Graham, J. K., Cameron, J., Dombroski, K., Healy, S., Miller, E., & Community Economies Collective. (2017). *Cultivating community economies.* Retrieved February 28, 2019, from TheNextSystem.org website: https://thenextsystem.org/cultivating-community-economies.

Gibson-Graham, J. K., Cameron, J., & Healy, S. (2013). *Take back the economy.* Minneapolis: University of Minnesota Press.

Goddard, R. (2001, June). Electronic fetal monitoring is not necessary for low risk labours. *BMJ, 322,* 1436–1437.

Greenfield, B. (2015). *Mom sues doctor over c-section fight: 'I was treated like a child'* . Retrieved from https://www.yahoo.com/news/mom-sues-doctor-over-c-section-fight-i-was-090037592.html.

Greer, G. (2011). *Shakespeare's wife.* ebook: A&C Black.

Gudeman, S., & Rivera, A. (1995). From care to house (Del coche a la casa). *American Anthropologist, 97*(2), 242–250.

Gupta, J. K., Hofmeyr, G. J., & Smyth, R. (2004). Position in the second stage of labour for women without epidural anaesthesia. *Cochrane Database of Systematic Reviews,* Issue 1. Art. No. CD002006. https://doi.org/10.1002/14651858. CD002006.pub2.

Haraway, D. (1990). *Simians, cyborgs, and women : The reinvention of nature*. New York: Routledge.

Haraway, D. (2008). Companion species, mis-recognition, and queer worlding. In N. Giffney & M. J. Hird (Eds.), *Queering the non/human*. Aldershot: Ashgate.

Heidegger, M. (1967). *What is a thing?*. Chicago: Henry Regnery Company.

Hoag, C. (2011). Assembling partial perspectives: Thoughts on the anthropology of bureaucracy. *Political and Legal Anthropology Critical Review, 34*(1), 81–94.

Hochschild, A. R. (2003). *The managed heart: Commercialization of human feeling* (20th anniversary ed.). Berkeley, CA: University of California Press.

Jackson, M., Dahlen, H., & Schmied, V. (2012). Birthing outside the system: Perspectives of risk amongst Australian women who have high risk homebirths. *Midwifery, 28*(5), 561–567.

Kedgley, S. J. (1996). *Mum's the word: The untold story of motherhood in New Zealand*. Auckland: Random House New Zealand.

Kitzinger, S. (2006). Birth as rape: There must be an end to 'just in case' obstetrics. *British Journal of Midwifery, 14*(9), 544–545. https://doi.org/10.12968/bjom.2006.14.9.21799.

Kitzinger, S. (2011). *Rediscovering birth*. London: Pinter and Martin Publishers.

Kristeva, J. (1980). Motherhood according to Giovanni Bellini. In *Desire in language: A semiotic approach to language and literature* (pp. 237–270). New York: Columbia University Press.

Latour, B. (2004). How to talk about the body? The normative dimension of science studies. *Body & Society, 10*(2–3), 205–229. https://doi.org/10.1177/1357034X04042943.

Latour, B. (2005). *Reassembling the social: An introduction to actor-network-theory*. Oxford and New York: Oxford University Press.

Law, J. (2004). *After method: Mess in social research*. London and New York: Routledge.

Leavitt, J. W. (1980). Birthing and anesthesia: The debate over twilight sleep. *Signs: Journal of Women in Culture and Society, 6*(1), 147–164.

Lerner, J. S., Li, Y., Valdesolo, P., & Kassam, K. S. (2015). Emotion and decision making. *Annual Review of Psychology, 66*(1), 799–823. https://doi.org/10.1146/annurev-psych-010213-115043.

Lewis, T., Amini, F., & Lannon, R. (2001). *A general theory of love*. New York: Vintage.

Lieberman, J. J. (1976). Childbirth practices: From darkness into light. *Journal of Obstetric, Gynecologic, & Neonatal Nursing, 5*(3), 41–45. https://doi.org/10.1111/j.1552-6909.1976.tb02306.x.

Longhurst, R. (2000). 'Corporeographies' of pregnancy: 'Bikini babes.' *Environment and Planning D: Society and Space, 18*(4), 453–472. https://doi.org/10.1068/d234.

Longhurst, R. (2004). *Bodies: Exploring fluid boundaries.* https://doi.org/10.4324/9780203193600.

Lothian, J. A. (2009). Safe, healthy birth: What every pregnant woman needs to know. *The Journal of Perinatal Education, 18*(3), 48–54. http://dx.doi.org.ez.library.latrobe.edu.au/10.1624/105812409X461225.

Lupton, D. (2012). 'Precious cargo': Foetal subjects, risk and reproductive citizenship. *Critical Public Health, 22*(3), 329–340. https://doi.org/10.1080/09581596.2012.657612.

MacColl, M.-R. (2009). *The birth wars: The conflict putting Australian women and babies at risk.* St Lucia and Brisbane: University of Queensland Press.

Madhok, S., Philips, A., & Wilson, K. (2013). Introduction. In *Gender, agency and coercion* (pp. 1–13). Basingstoke: Palgrave Macmillan.

Mardorossian, C. M. (2014). *Framing the rape victim: Gender and agency reconsidered.* New Brunswick, NJ and London: Rutgers University Press.

Martin, K. A. (2003). Giving birth like a girl. *Gender & Society, 17*(1), 54–72. https://doi.org/10.1177/0891243202238978.

McCourt, C., & Dykes, F. (2010). From tradition to modernity: Time and childbirth in historical perspective. In *Childbirth, midwifery and concepts of time* (pp. 17–36). Oxford: Berghahn Books.

McKinnon, K. (2017). Naked scholarship: Prefiguring a new world through uncertain development geographies. *Geographical Research, 55*(3), 344–349. https://doi.org/10.1111/1745-5871.12196.

Medcom. (2008). *Obstetrical nursing, electronic fetal monitoring.* Cypress, CA: Medcom.

Mills, C. (2014). Making fetal persons: Fetal homicide, ultrasound, and the normative significance of birth. *Philosophia, 4*(1), 88–107.

Mills, C. (2015). The case of the missing hand: Gender, disability, and bodily norms in selective termination. *Hypatia, 30*(1), 82–96.

Mol, A. (2002). *The body multiple: Ontology in medical practice.* Durham: Duke University Press.

Mol, A. (2008). *The logic of care: Health and the problem of patient choice.* London and New York: Routledge.

Mol, A., & Law, J. (2004). Embodied action, enacted bodies: The example of hypoglycaemia. *Body & Society, 10*(2–3), 43–62. https://doi.org/10.1177/1357034X04042932.

Morrow, O., & Dombroski, K. (2015). Enacting a postcapitalist politics through the sites and practices of life's work. In *Precarious worlds: Contested geographies of social reproduction.* Athens, GA: University of Georgia Press.

Moscucci, O. (2003). Holistic obstetrics: The origins of "natural childbirth" in Britain. *Postgraduate Medical Journal, 79*(929), 168–173. https://doi.org/10.1136/pmj.79.929.168.

OBOS Pregnancy and Birth Contributors. (2014). *Models of maternity care.* Retrieved May 24, 2019, from Our Bodies Ourselves website: https://www. ourbodiesourselves.org/book-excerpts/health-article/models-of-maternity-care/.

O'Brien, M. (1981). *The politics of reproduction.* Boston, London, and Henley: Routledge & Kegan Paul.

Odent, M. (2009). Masculinisation of the birth environment. *Journal of Prenatal and Perinatal Psychology and Health, 23*(3), 185–191.

Oxford English Dictionary. (2019). *Work.* Retrieved from Oxford Living Dictionaries—English website: https://en.oxforddictionaries.com/definition/work.

Paice, E., & Smith, D. (2009). Bullying of trainee doctors is a patient safety issue. *The Clinical Teacher, 6*(1), 13–17. https://doi.org/10.1111/j.1743-498X. 2008.00251.x.

Paterno, M. T., McElroy, K., & Regan, M. (2016). Electronic fetal monitoring and cesarean birth: A scoping review. *Birth, 43*(4), 277–284. https://doi.org/10. 1111/birt.12247.

Pérez D'Gregorio, R. (2010). Obstetric violence: A new legal term introduced in Venezuela. *International Journal of Gynecology & Obstetrics, 111*(3), 201–202. https://doi.org/10.1016/j.ijgo.2010.09.002.

Pettker, C. M., & Campbell, K. H. (2012). Antepartum fetal assessment. In Christine A. Gleason & S. U. Devaskar (Eds.), *Avery's diseases of the newborn* (9th ed., pp. 129–139). https://doi.org/10.1016/B978-1-4377-0134-0.10013-7.

Reed, R., Sharman, R., & Inglis, C. (2017). Women's descriptions of childbirth trauma relating to care provider actions and interactions. *BMC Pregnancy and Childbirth, 17*(1). https://doi.org/10.1186/s12884-016-1197-0.

Reid, A. J., & Harris, N. L. (1988). Alternative birth positions. *Canadian Family Physician, 34*, 1993–1998.

Richland, S. (2008). Birth rape: Another midwife's story. *Midwifery Today*, Spring, 42–43.

Rose, M. (2018). Consciousness as claiming: Practice and habit in an enigmatic world. *Environment and Planning D: Society and Space, 36*(6), 1120–1135. https://doi.org/10.1177/0263775818784754.

Royal College of Midwives. (2017). RCM and RCOG publish joint statement on electronic fetal monitoring. *RCM.* Retrieved February 23, 2019, from https://www.rcm.org.uk/news-views-and-analysis/news/rcm-and-rcog-publish-joint-statement-on-electronic-fetal-monitoring.

Ruddick, S. (1989). *Maternal thinking: Towards a politics of peace.* New York: Ballantine Books.

Russel, K. (1997). A value-theoretic approach to childbirth. In *Materialist feminism: A reader in class, difference and women's lives* (pp. 328–344). New York and London: Routledge.

Sadler, M., Santos, M. J., Ruiz-Berdún, D., Rojas, G. L., Skoko, E., Gillen, P., & Clausen, J. A. (2016). Moving beyond disrespect and abuse: Addressing the structural dimensions of obstetric violence. *Reproductive Health Matters,* 24(47), 47–55. https://doi.org/10.1016/j.rhm.2016.04.002.

Saling, E., & Dräger, M. (2014). Fetal heart rate activity and measurements of labor activity. In *The beginnings of perinatal medicine* (pp. 5–21). Munich, Germany and Boston, MA: De Gruyter.

Sartwelle, T. (2012). Electronic fetal monitoring: A bridge too far. *Journal of Legal Medicine, 33*(3), 313–379.

Schipper, B. (2011). *Julia Kristeva and feminist thought.* Edinburgh: Edinburgh University Press.

Schore, A., & McIntosh, J. (2011). Family law and the neuroscience of attachment. *Family Court Review, 49*(3), 501–512. https://doi.org/10.1111/j.1744-1617.2011.01387.x.

Sedgwick, E. K. (2002). *Touching feeling: Affect, pedagogy, performativity.* Durham, NC: Duke University Press.

Shabot, S. C. (2016). Making loud bodies "feminine": A feminist-phenomenological analysis of obstetric violence. *Human Studies, 39*(2), 231–247. https://doi.org/10.1007/s10746-015-9369-x.

Sheikh, S., Ganesaratnam, I., & Jan, H. (2013). The birth of forceps. *JRSM Short Reports, 4*(7), 1–4. https://doi.org/10.1177/2042533313478412.

Simonds, W. (2002). Watching the clock: Keeping time during pregnancy, birth, and postpartum experiences. *Social Science & Medicine, 55*(4), 559–570. https://doi.org/10.1016/S0277-9536(01)00196-4.

Simpson, M., Schmied, V., Dickson, C., & Dahlen, H. (2018). Postnatal post-traumatic stress: An integrative review. *Women and Birth, 31*(5), 367–379. https://doi.org/10.1016/j.wombi.2017.12.003.

Slovic, P., Finucane, M. L., Peters, E., & MacGregor, D. G. (2004). Risk as analysis and risk as feelings: Some thoughts about affect, reason, risk, and rationality. *Risk Analysis, 24*(2), 311–322. https://doi.org/10.1111/j.0272-4332.2004.00433.x.

Smith, J., Plaat, F., & Fisk, N. (2008). The natural caesarean: A woman-centred technique. *BJOG: An International Journal of Obstetrics & Gynaecology, 115*(8), 1037–1042. https://doi.org/10.1111/j.1471-0528.2008.01777.x.

Spilsted, M. (2019). *Hypnobirthing Australia.* Retrieved from https://hypnobirthingaustralia.com.au/whatishypnobirthing/.

Stephens, J. (2011). *Confronting postmaternalism.* New York: Columbia University Press.

Stephenson, N., McLeod, K., & Mills, C. (2016). Ambiguous encounters, uncertain foetuses: Women's experiences of obstetric ultrasound. *Feminist Review, 113*(1), 17–33. https://doi.org/10.1057/fr.2016.6.

Thompson, E. P. (1967). Time, work-discipline, and industrial capitalism. *The Past and Present Society, 38*, 56–97.

Thornton, C., Schmied, V., Dennis, C.-L., Barnett, B., & Dahlen, H. (2013). *Maternal deaths in NSW (2000–2006) from nonmedical causes (suicide and trauma) in the first year following birth* [Research article]. https://doi.org/10.1155/2013/623743.

Underhill-Sem, Y. (2001). Maternities in 'out-of-the-way' places: Epistemological possibilities for retheorising population geography. *International Journal of Population Geography, 7*(6), 447–460. https://doi.org/10.1002/ijpg.241.

United States Patent Office. (1942). 'Hospital Bed', Patent 2,275,973. Cattanooga, Tenn: Marchbanks.

WHO, UNICEF, UNFPA, World Bank Group, & United Nations Population Division. (2015). *Trends in maternal mortality: 1990 to 2015*. Retrieved from https://www.who.int/reproductivehealth/publications/monitoring/maternal-mortality-2015/en/.

Wielgosz, J., Goldberg, S. B., Kral, T. R. A., Dunne, J. D., & Davidson, R. J. (2019). Mindfulness meditation and psychopathology. *Annual Review of Clinical Psychology, 15*(1). https://doi.org/10.1146/annurev-clinpsy-021815-093423.

World Health Organization. (2014). *Delayed umbilical cord clamping for improved maternal and infant health and nutrition outcomes—Guideline*. Retrieved from https://www.who.int/nutrition/publications/guidelines/cord_clamping/en/.

World Health Organization. (2015). *WHO statement on caesarean section rates*. Retrieved from http://www.who.int/reproductivehealth/publications/maternal_perinatal_health/cs-statement/en/.

World Health Organization. (2018a). *WHO recommendations: Intrapartum care for a positive birth experience*. Retrieved from http://www.ncbi.nlm.nih.gov/books/NBK513809/.

World Health Organization. (2018b). *WHO recommendation on duration of the first stage of labour*. Retrieved from https://extranet.who.int/rhl/topics/preconception-pregnancy-childbirth-and-postpartum-care/care-during-childbirth/care-during-labour-1st-stage/who-recommendation-duration-first-stage-labour.

Wright, L. (1962). *Warm and snug: The history of the bed*. London: Routledge & Kegan Paul.

Zerilli, L. (1992). A process without a subject: Simone de Beauvoir and Julia Kristeva on maternity. *Signs: Journal of Women in Culture and Society, 18*(1), 111–135.

INDEX